D0074939

Knowledge Acquisition for Expert Systems

A Practical Handbook

Knowledge Acquisition for Expert Systems

A Practical Handbook

Edited by

ALISON L. KIDD

Hewlett Packard Laboratories
Bristol, England

Plenum Press • New York and London

Library of Congress Cataloging in Publication Data

Knowledge acquisition for expert systems.

Bibliography: p.
Includes index.
1. Expert systems (Computer science). 2. System design. I. Kidd, Alison L.
QA76.76.E95K554   1987   006.3′3   87-12274
ISBN 0-306-42454-1

© 1987 Plenum Press, New York
A Division of Plenum Publishing Corporation
233 Spring Street, New York, N.Y. 10013

Printed in the United States of America

Contributors

Joost Breuker, Department of Social Science Informatics, University of Amsterdam, 1016 BS Amsterdam, The Netherlands

John Fox, Biomedical Computing Unit, Imperial Cancer Research Fund, London WC2A 3PX, England

Brian R. Gaines, Department of Computer Science, University of Calgary, Calgary, Alberta, Canada T2N 1N4

John G. Gammack, MRC Applied Psychology Unit, Cambridge CB2 2EF, England

Melvyn F. Greaves, The Leukaemia Research Fund Centre, Institute for Cancer Research, London SW3 6JB, England

Anna Hart, Lancashire Polytechnic, Preston PR1 2TQ, England

Leslie Johnson, Department of Computer Science, Brunel University, Uxbridge, Middlesex UB8 3PH, England

Nancy E. Johnson, Department of Computer Science, Brunel University, Uxbridge, Middlesex UB8 3PH, England

Jerome P. Kassirer, Department of Medicine, Tufts University School of Medicine, Boston, Massachusetts 02111

Alison L. Kidd, Hewlett Packard Laboratories, Stoke Gifford, Bristol BS12 6QZ, England

Benjamin Kuipers, Department of Computer Sciences, University of Texas at Austin, Austin, Texas 78712

Christopher D. Myers, Biomedical Computing Unit, Imperial Cancer Research Fund, London WC2A 3PX, England, and Department of Microbiology, University of Texas, Dallas, Texas 75235

Susan Pegram, The Leukaemia Research Fund Centre, Institute for Cancer Research, London SW3 6JB, England

Mildred L. G. Shaw, Department of Computer Science, University of Calgary, Calgary, Alberta, Canada T2N 1N4

Bob Wielinga, Department of Social Science Informatics, University of Amsterdam, 1016 BS Amsterdam, The Netherlands

Preface

Building an expert system involves eliciting, analyzing, and interpreting the knowledge that a human expert uses when solving problems. Experience has shown that this process of "knowledge acquisition" is both difficult and time consuming and is often a major bottleneck in the production of expert systems. Unfortunately, an adequate theoretical basis for knowledge acquisition has not yet been established. This requires a classification of knowledge domains and problem-solving tasks and an improved understanding of the relationship between knowledge structures in human and machine.

In the meantime, expert system builders need access to information about the techniques currently being employed and their effectiveness in different applications. The aim of this book, therefore, is to draw on the experience of AI scientists, cognitive psychologists, and knowledge engineers in discussing particular acquisition techniques and providing practical advice on their application. Each chapter provides a detailed description of a particular technique or methodology applied within a selected task domain. The relative strengths and weaknesses of the technique are summarized at the end of each chapter with some suggested guidelines for its use.

We hope that this book will not only serve as a practical handbook for expert system builders, but also be of interest to AI and cognitive scientists who are seeking to develop a theory of knowledge acquisition for expert systems.

Alison L. Kidd

Bristol, England

Contents

CHAPTER 3

KNOWLEDGE ACQUISITION BY ANALYSIS OF VERBATIM PROTOCOLS

Benjamin Kuipers and Jerome P. Kassirer

CHAPTER 4

A SYSTEMATIC STUDY OF KNOWLEDGE BASE REFINEMENT IN THE
DIAGNOSIS OF LEUKEMIA

*John Fox, Christopher D. Myers, Melvyn F. Greaves, and
Susan Pegram*

CHAPTER 5

KNOWLEDGE ELICITATION INVOLVING TEACHBACK INTERVIEWING

Leslie Johnson and Nancy E. Johnson

CHAPTER 6

AN INTERACTIVE KNOWLEDGE-ELICITATION TECHNIQUE USING
PERSONAL CONSTRUCT TECHNOLOGY

Mildred L. G. Shaw and Brian R. Gaines

CHAPTER 7

DIFFERENT TECHNIQUES AND DIFFERENT ASPECTS ON DECLARATIVE KNOWLEDGE

John G. Gammack

CHAPTER 8

ROLE OF INDUCTION IN KNOWLEDGE ELICITATION

Anna Hart

1

Knowledge Acquisition
An Introductory Framework

ALISON L. KIDD

1. INTRODUCTION

Knowledge acquisition (KA) is a crucial stage in the development of an expert system. As a process, it involves eliciting, analyzing, and interpreting the knowledge that a human expert uses when solving a particular problem and then transforming this knowledge into a suitable machine representation. KA is critical since the power and utility of the resulting expert system depend on the quality of the underlying representation of expert knowledge. The aim of this book is to provide the builders of expert systems with some practical advice on what KA involves and some of the methodologies and techniques that have been developed to aid its effectiveness.

The fact that KA has proved such a major stumbling block in the production of expert systems is not surprising. To solve the problem of KA in any real sense would entail answering some fundamental questions, not only in AI, but also in psychology and the philosophy of science. For example:

- What is the relationship between knowledge and language?
- How can we characterise different domains of knowledge?
- What constitutes a theory of human problem solving?

ALISON L. KIDD • Hewlett Packard Laboratories, Stoke Gifford, Bristol BS12 6QZ, England.

The fact that KA as a process now has its own name and has received so much recent attention in AI does not make these underlying questions any easier to answer. Until we have some answers, there is no hope that AI research can produce one "magical" technique that solves the KA problem. Any claims that such a technique exists (e.g., Michie and Johnston, 1985) are fundamentally misguided.

This book was designed to fill a gap in the existing literature on KA between, on the one hand, AI research papers that describe only scantily the techniques employed in acquiring the knowledge for any expert system and, on the other hand, the large body of literature describing techniques developed within cognitive and behavioral psychology. The latter, although seemingly relevant, have rarely been applied to expert system applications or even described in terms that system builders can easily interpret and exploit.

Each chapter of the book provides a detailed description of a particular KA technique or methodology, applied within a selected task domain. The relative strengths and weaknesses of the technique are summarized at the end of each chapter with some suggested guidelines for its use. Some of the chapters are written from the standpoint of the AI scientist, interested primarily in building a powerful working system to simulate some expert task (e.g., Kuipers and Kassirer, Fox *et al.*). Others are written from the standpoint of the psychologist applying some well-tried psychological technique to an expert system style application (e.g., Shaw and Gaines, Gammack).

By way of introduction, this opening chapter makes a series of points that clarify the purpose of the KA process and outline what it involves. The aim is, first, to uncover some common misconceptions in the way KA is currently described and practiced and, second, to provide a theoretical framework that will help readers to interpret and assess the value of the diverse set of techniques described in the following chapters, in relation to their own KA requirements. Many of the theoretical issues raised in this chapter are discussed in greater depth by individual authors. However, all the opinions expressed in this chapter are not necessarily shared by my fellow authors.

2. THE KNOWLEDGE ACQUISITION PROCESS: MINING IS A MISGUIDED ANALOGY

A popular view of KA has been to consider experts' heads as being filled with bits of knowledge and the problem of KA as being one of "mining those jewels of knowledge out of their heads one by one"

(Feigenbaum and McCorduck, 1983). The underlying assumption is that some magical one-to-one correspondence exists between the verbal comments made by an expert during an elicitation session and real items of knowledge that are buried deep within his head (Kidd and Welbank, 1984). Once these comments are transcribed onto a piece of paper, they are considered to be nuggets of the truth about that domain. The analogy is misleading; there is no *truth* in that sense. Rather, it is the case that KA involves the following:

1. Employing a technique to elicit data (usually verbal) from the expert.
2. Interpreting these verbal data (more or less skillfully) in order to infer what might be the expert's underlying knowledge and reasoning processes.
3. Using this interpretation to guide the construction of some model or language that describes (more or less accurately) the expert's knowledge and performance. Interpretation of further data is guided in turn by this evolving model (Johnson, 1985).

Knowledge engineers need to recognize that this is the basic process in which they are engaging and that the techniques described in this book are ways of helping them carry out this process more accurately and effectively.

3. KNOWLEDGE DOMAINS: CAPTURING OR CREATING A LANGUAGE

In the past 10 years, expert systems have been constructed in a wide variety of domains. Even within this book, the list includes domains as dissimilar as leukemia diagnosis, air-conditioning design, children's arithmetic, and the selection of college students. Unfortunately, AI currently has no formal (or even informal) characterization of different knowledge domains. Only as we develop such a characterization, will it be possible to identify meaningfully and to classify KA techniques in relation to different domains and tasks. An approach to increasing our present understanding of this classification is proposed in section 4.

In the meantime, there are two fundamental questions that knowledge engineers can ask about any domain now, the answers to which are critical in determining (1) the suitability of that domain for developing a successful expert system and (2) the type of KA that is necessary for developing such a system.

What language do humans possess for representing and reasoning within this domain? (Is it formally defined? If not, how stable and well-agreed is it?)

Example Class 1: Mathematics, Geometry, Programming Languages. In this class of domains, humans have already developed a formal language for representation and reasoning; i.e., axioms, semantics, and syntax have been defined. KA for such domains should therefore be straightforward, involving the capture of some subset of this language and mapping it into an appropriate machine equivalent. The only difficult part of the KA process is discovering and describing how the expert maps this formal language onto any real-world problem. This activity is no longer formally defined, and here the knowledge engineer will have to create a language to describe the process.

Example Class 2: Medicine, Chemistry, Electronic Equipment Design and Diagnosis. Humans have not yet developed a formal language for domains in this class. At the deepest level, functionality is described in terms of physical laws, but these are hypotheses, not axioms: They may have a basis in deeper theory and be subject to error (Clancey, 1986). However, humans have developed a fairly stable, well-agreed language for representing and reasoning about such domains. KA therefore involves capturing the essence of this language and then systematizing it for machine purposes.

Example Class 3: Applications Software, Management, Marketing. Domains in this class do not currently have a stable, well-agreed language for representation or reasoning. They lack a coherent underlying theory. For example, when an applications programmer is required to develop a new electronic mail system, he first has to develop his own theory of electronic mail before writing the software to realize this theory in his own idiosyncratic way. As a result, such domains present the worst problems for expert system development because KA must involve the creation of a "new" language (and therefore an implicit theory) that will adequately support reasoning within the domain. This new language is likely to be the subject of continuous negotiation with both experts and users even when the expert system is developed. Surprisingly, however, this class of domain is proving increasingly popular for expert system development, e.g., electronic mail advice systems. Presumably this is because such domains present the biggest problems to human reasoning simply because they lack an agreed language or any underlying theory. Knowledge engineers need to be very aware of these problems and of what KA in such a domain must involve.

Is there an existing machine representation that can adequately support the human's domain language?

Example Class 4: Spatial Reasoning Tasks, e.g., Stick-and-Ball Models of Molecules. In some domains, humans have developed a fairly formal and powerful language for reasoning about a class of difficult problems, but such a language is currently unsupportable with state-of-the-art machine representation techniques. The main thrust of the KA process in such a domain is to develop a new machine language that can adequately capture the power of the existing human language.*

4. TASKS: DEFINING THE PROBLEM THAT THE EXPERT SYSTEM IS DESIGNED TO SOLVE

The aim of an expert system is not merely to capture a static representation of some knowledge domain but to simulate a particular problem-solving task (or tasks) carried out within that domain. A generic set of such tasks has been identified by Hayes-Roth *et al.* (1984) and is now widely referenced. This list comprises the following:

INTERPRETATION   Inferring situation descriptions from sensor data.

PREDICTION   Inferring likely consequences of a given situation.

DIAGNOSIS   Inferring system malfunctions from observables.

DESIGN   Configuring objects under constraints.

PLANNING   Designing actions.

MONITORING   Comparing observations to plan vulnerabilities.

DEBUGGING   Prescribing remedies for malfunctions.

REPAIR   Executing a plan to administer a prescribed remedy.

INSTRUCTION   Diagnosing, debugging, and repairing student behavior.

CONTROL   Interpreting, predicting, repairing, and monitoring system behaviors.

The utility, and indeed validity, of these categories is questionable for three reasons: (1) What appears to be an inherent property of a real-world problem may rather be a property of how AI programs currently

---

*I would like to acknowledge the contribution of my colleague, Bill Sharpe, to many of the ideas discussed in this section.

solve that problem. (2) There is evidence that the same task in two different domains may actually involve solving different kinds of problem, e.g., medical versus electronic diagnosis (Clancey, 1985). (3) Any one of the task categories listed above may, in practice, incorporate a subset of other tasks; e.g., diagnosis may include elements of planning or prediction.

Even if we do take the Hayes-Roth categories as they stand, AI still lacks a theory that will map existing AI tools or shells onto the categories of tasks that they can solve (see Bennett, 1985; Clancey, 1985, 1986). This is a sad state of affairs after more than 10 years of wide-ranging experience in the applied AI field. For example, when presented with a given AI tool (e.g., EMYCIN), we are still hard pressed to say what kinds of problems it can be used to solve well (Clancey, 1985). The emphasis has been biased too much toward a "performance" approach to AI (Hall and Kibler, 1985), where research has been oriented entirely toward achieving impressive levels of performance on different tasks with minimal or no theoretical underpinning. Consequently, we are now in a position where we often cannot explain why any system does, or does not, perform successfully on a particular task or predict other problems where it might be successfully applied (cf. Nilsson, 1980). The most AI can offer are collections of rather vague and poorly understood heuristics for selecting appropriate domains; e.g., "The task is neither too easy (taking a human expert less than a few minutes) nor too difficult (requiring more than a few hours for an expert)" (Prerau, 1985).

If it is to have a successful future, then the emphasis within applied AI must change toward a more formal, top-down approach to system building (see Hall and Kibler, 1985). This obviously impacts directly on the process of KA because it requires, first, that the knowledge engineer should identify and isolate the particular problem-solving task that he wishes to simulate. Second, he should attempt to analyze and then describe the types of knowledge necessary to solve that problem independently of any particular implementation (Clancey, 1985; Marr, 1977; Newell, 1982). The more complete such a "knowledge-level" description (Newell, 1982) is, the more powerful it will be in providing the following:

- A once-for-all description of what it means to solve a particular class of problem. Different, more efficient ways of implementing the solution may be developed over time but the "knowledge-level" description will not change.
- An intermediate representation of the knowledge that can be used during the KA process to help guide elicitation and interpretation of the resulting verbal data and decisions about an appropriate

machine representation. For fuller treatment of this point, see both the Breuker and Wielinga and the Johnson and Johnson chapters in this volume.

- A formal specification of what the finished expert system should be able to do. This should militate against the too-prevalent "candy-box" approach to AI, where tools and shells offer an ever-increasing number of new and exciting facilities without any knowledge of either what to use these facilities for or which ones, if any, are actually necessary requirements for solving any problem. Rather, the further development of such fancy facilities should be put on one side while we attempt to identify some of the minimal "dietary requirements" for solving any problem (Johnson, 1986).
- A framework for addressing the important problems of validity, completeness, and maintenance of expert knowledge bases.
- A basis for explaining why (or why not) a system is successful in a particular application and reliably predicting where else it might be successfully applied.

I wish to underline two practical points here for those who are involved in the commercial development of expert systems:

1. The approach advocated here is *not* one that is relevant only to academic research. If a commercial company wishes to exploit expert systems technology successfully and on a significant scale, then this can happen only if the system builders move beyond the current simplistic one-off performance approach ("Let's see if we can build a useful system using shell X. . . .") to a position where they have a knowledge-level description of the problem solved by any tool that allows them to exploit that tool in a range of similar applications.
2. It is not necessary to develop a complete formal theory of any problem for this approach to be useful. At the least, a weak theory should help in classifying some of the different types of knowledge necessary to solve a particular problem and thus facilitate the process of analyzing and interpreting data from knowledge elicitation interviews or protocols. Without any such theory, it is rather like the vain hope that a room full of monkeys let loose on a batch of typewriters will eventually come up with the works of Shakespeare (Adams, 1979)!

The Breuker and Weilinga chapter in this volume describes a well-developed and tested methodology for adopting this more formal approach to KA.

5. SYSTEM MODALITY: DEFINING THE SET OF TASKS

For purposes of clarity in Section 4, I described only the simple case where a knowledge-level description is developed for a single problem-solving task that had been isolated for simulation. Unfortunately, when one is building expert systems for practical use, the situation becomes much more complex. A medical expert, for example, does not simply carry out diagnostic reasoning. Rather, this reasoning is part of some functional role (or "modality") that he fulfills within his domain of expertise. For example, at any time he may be providing advice in his role as consultant to his patients or be providing explanations in his role as medical tutor to his juniors.

This point has constantly been overlooked in the development of expert systems and may largely account for their lack of success in practical applications despite their problem-solving prowess (Coombs and Alty, 1984; Kidd, 1985a). As Breuker and Wielinga (this volume) point out, the distinction between roles (or modalities) and problem-solving tasks has not even been recognized. They cite the example of the Hayes-Roth *et al.* list shown in Section 4, where, for instance, "Instruction" (a modality) is included alongside "Diagnosis" (a task). This is a crucial point because changing the modality of an expert system is not (as was originally thought) merely a case of adding a different modality-specific front end onto an existing knowledge base. Clancey's unsuccessful attempts to convert MYCIN into a tutoring system illustrate this point most clearly. He found that a complete reconstruction of the underlying knowledge base was required (e.g., Clancey and Letsinger, 1981). The Breuker and Wielinga chapter discusses this point in more detail.

In designing any expert system, therefore, the first step must be to decide on the appropriate modality for that system. If, as is the case in the majority of expert systems, the desired modality is one of a domain consultant, then the next step should be to identify the set of problem-solving tasks that are the minimal requirements of a consultant in the selected domain. One way of doing this is by recording and analyzing naturally occurring consultation dialogues between experts and their clients. Analysis of a number of such dialogues (Coombs and Alty, 1984; Kidd, 1985a, 1985b; Pollack *et al.*, 1982) has clearly shown that, independent of the domain, consultation includes the following tasks:

1. Negotiating with the user an adequate formulation of his problem in domain terms. This is a critical phase in any problem-solving process (Mitroff and Featheringham, 1974), but current expert systems fail to address it at all.

2. Answering a range of user questions about the domain, e.g.,
   Why did X happen?
   How can I achieve Y?
   Will Z achieve Y?

   Answering such questions may well cut across, or at least involve a complex interaction of, the task types listed by Hayes-Roth *et al.* (1983).
3. Communicating advice to the user in a form that is focused, intelligible, and convincing. The single-solution output and trace-style explanations of current expert systems do not match this requirement.

For more detailed treatment of these tasks, see Kidd (1985a, 1985b).

6. USERS: ACQUIRING THEIR KNOWLEDGE

In any interactive expert system, the user is an active agent in the problem-solving process (Kidd, 1985b). In the past, the design of both expert systems and intelligent tutoring systems (Sleeman and Brown, 1982) has tended to be based on the assumption that the system, in some sense, contains the true model of the domain and the aim is to transfer this truth into the empty head of some passive user! Rather, it is the case that any user (or student), however little he knows about the domain, will still be actively acquiring and organizing the expert's knowledge for some purpose of his own. This is why the negotiation process outlined above is so important. There are always two models of the domain, the system's and the user's. Neither is "true" in some objective sense, but each may be organized for different purposes.

Since this is the case, a key part of the KA process must be to analyze certain key aspects of prospective users. Too often, consideration of users is a last-minute icing on the cake. Rather, I would argue that the user's needs constitute the minimal "dietary requirements" for any useful expert system, and therefore KA should include the following:

1. Identifying the different classes of users likely to use the system and their different needs.
2. Analyzing user requirements—e.g., What are the common classes of problems and questions? What advice does the user require and in what form? (e.g., Does he usually have his own idea of a solution and only require a critique from the expert? Does he

need to have a set of alternative solutions with pros and cons spelt out?) What type of justification does he require?

3. Analyzing what types of knowledge the user brings to bear on the problem-solving process. Recent research indicates that these include the user's goals within the domain; his constraints on acceptable solutions (e.g., time, availability, cost); his own model of the current problem; his own model of the type of problems that the system can solve for him (see Kidd, 1985a, 1985b).

Unfortunately, we do not yet understand how to incorporate user knowledge of this type in order to create a truly cooperative problem-solving process between the system and the user. However, acquiring this user knowledge is still critical for enabling good design decisions about the proposed system.

7. AN ALTERNATIVE APPROACH: IDENTIFYING WEAKNESSES IN HUMAN REASONING

The common aim of expert systems has been to simulate those elements of human reasoning in which human experts are highly competent. The systems are then usually applied in a decision support role to help other lesser experts solve the same problems. A recent paper by Woods (1986) proposes that a more effective way to employ AI technology would be in supporting those aspects of reasoning at which most humans (experts or not) are weak, as a result of their in-built cognitive limitations. Examples of such weaknesses in human reasoning include the following:

- Fixation or preservation effects in an operator's assessment in the state of some process (Norman, 1986; Woods, 1984).
- Weaknesses in counterfactual reasoning; e.g., "Would Y have occurred if X had not?"
- Failing to take into account negative evidence for a hypothesis (Elstein et al., 1978).
- Data sampling/information acquisition problems: Can the user find and integrate the "right" data for the current context and task (Woods, 1986)?
- Thinking through the consequences of complex interactions.

Woods is suggesting that the human and the expert system should be conceived as a joint cognitive system. To adopt this approach, KA would focus on analyzing what makes for competence and/or incompetence within a particular problem-solving task and then aim to use this information to design reasoning systems that support the cognitive demands of the domain in a way that complements, not copies, human abilities.

8. CONCLUDING GUIDELINES FOR KNOWLEDGE ENGINEERS

The complex problems of knowledge acquisition cannot be fully solved, or even explained, until fundamental issues such as the nature of different knowledge domains and different problem-solving tasks are better understood.

In the meantime, the following guidelines for KA can be drawn up. They are important for commercial expert system development as well as AI research. These guidelines may serve as a framework for interpreting the diverse set of KA techniques described in the subsequent chapters and assessing their relative value for any particular application.

1. Knowledge engineers should appreciate the basic characteristics of the KA process: (a) Any data that are elicited from a human expert have to be interpreted as to what underlying knowledge or processes they imply; (b) the system knowledge base is a model (or theory) of the expert's domain knowledge that is constructed by the knowledge engineer.

2. The nature (and difficulty) of the KA process is directly dependent on whether the human language in a chosen domain is formal or, at least, well agreed among experts. Knowledge engineers can use this attribute both to evaluate different applications and to guide the KA process within any chosen domain.

3. Knowledge engineers should aim to formulate a knowledge-level description of the selected problem-solving task. This will provide a specification of the minimal requirements for the proposed expert system and a guide to the types of knowledge to be acquired. It should also enable the successful generalization of AI techniques to related problem areas.

4. At an early stage, knowledge engineers need to decide on the appropriate modality for the proposed expert system, e.g., automated expert, consultant, or tutor. This will enable them to identify the set of problem-solving tasks required by the system.

5. In any interactive expert system, the user is an active agent in the problem-solving process. Analyzing user requirements and user domain knowledge should therefore be a key part of KA.

6. If the role of the proposed system is decision support, then knowledge engineers should consider identifying specific weaknesses in the expert human reasoning process and designing a system to complement these.

If knowledge engineers seek to adopt the more formal, theory-based, approach to KA advocated in these guidelines and subsequently report their efforts across a variety of application domains, then this accumulated wisdom will significantly advance our understanding of fundamental AI questions about both the nature of and the relationship among domains, tasks, and AI technologies. Only by adopting such an approach can we hope to move beyond the production of poorly defined heuristics on knowledge acquisition to a theoretically sound methodology that will guarantee future efficiency and success.

9. BRIEF OVERVIEW OF CHAPTERS

CHAPTER 2: JOOST BREUKER AND BOB WIELINGA

The basis for the Breuker and Wielinga chapter is the need for a principled and systematic methodology for expert system development. This is in contrast to the currently adopted "rapid prototyping" approach. The authors describe a methodology, KADS (Knowledge Acquisition and Document Structuring), which they have developed to meet this need. KADS consists of three cycles of knowledge analysis and elicitation; these are orientation, problem identification, and problem analysis. In parallel with these analyses are typical elicitation techniques that can be employed at each stage. The aim of KADS is to describe the basic architecture of the expert system, including its modality. It also enables early feasibility estimates of the developing system and provides documentation. The KADS methodology has largely been implemented as a knowledge-based interactive support tool for knowledge engineers. Its use is discussed in two test domains: commercial wine making and air-conditioning design.

CHAPTER 3: BENJAMIN KUIPERS AND JEROME P. KASSIRER

In the first part of this chapter, Kuipers and Kassirer demonstrate a methodology for collecting and analyzing observations of experts at work in order to discover the conceptual framework used for a particular domain. In the second part, they develop a representation for qualitative knowledge of the structure and behavior of a mechanism. The qualitative simulation process is given a qualitative structural description of a mechanism and some initialization information and produces a detailed description of the mechanism's behavior. The simulation process has been fully implemented and, in this chapter, the results are demonstrated for a particular disease mechanism in nephrology.

CHAPTER 4: JOHN FOX, CHRISTOPHER D. MYERS, MELVYN F. GREAVES, AND SUSAN PEGRAM

The authors of this chapter are primarily concerned with developing a working expert system for test interpretation in leukemia diagnosis. They describe an informal method of knowledge elicitation based on analysis of spoken commentaries from the expert while he solves a set of test cases. Verbatim transcripts of the tapes are made and a systematic approach to knowledge base development and quality control are explored. The material for the knowledge base is extracted from the transcripts in three stages: highlighting and extraction of apparently "substantive" information, simplification of this information to represent basic relationships, and refinement into a table of "If . . . then" rules. The expert system knowledge base is then built up by adding rules from this table in a series of distinct stages. At each stage, the performance of the knowledge base is systematically assessed by a process of direct comparison with the expert's performance data.

CHAPTER 5: LESLIE JOHNSON AND NANCY E. JOHNSON

Johnson and Johnson take the theoretical stance that expert systems design requires more than a model of "good as expert" performance; rather, it requires a model of expert "competence." The authors are therefore interested in ways of capturing the expert's conceptual structure, not just his procedural skills. They describe a technique that centers on a program of semistructured interviews based on a methodology derived from Pask's conversation theory. Interview data are treated as qualitative data to be analyzed from various perspectives. They employ a representational device, known as Systemic Grammar Networks, for expressing these analyses and for mediating between interviews and AI representation schemes. The device allows the principled selection of a representation scheme that will best express the model of competence. They describe an evaluation of this technique in two domains: children's arithmetic and VLSI design.

CHAPTER 6: MILDRED L. G. SHAW AND BRIAN R. GAINES

In this chapter, Shaw and Gaines describe a methodology for knowledge elicitation that has been implemented in a suite of computer programs that interact with experts and enable them to express the constructs underlying their knowledge. The methodology is based on Kelly's personal construct psychology, Checkland's soft systems analysis, and Pask's conversation theory. The suite of programs described uses interactive elicitation of repertory grids to elicit knowledge from experts and entailment analysis to derive rules with which to prime expert system shells. Examples are given of the programs in action in the domain of accounting needs of a company.

CHAPTER 7: JOHN G. GAMMACK

In this chapter, Gammack describes and evaluates a range of psychological techniques for discovering the expert's conceptual knowledge about a domain, including terms of reference and their usual intended meaning, relationships perceived among these domain concepts, and organizational structure giving them coherence for the expert. The approach described takes four consecutive phases: eliciting component terms to be used for construction, eliciting some structure for those terms, formally representing that structure, and, finally, transforming that representation to be used for some selected purpose. The psychological techniques Gammack considers include tutorial interviewing, card sorting, multidimensional scaling, repertory grids, a matrix technique, and proximity analysis. These are used to elicit different aspects of the expert's conceptual structure for a test domain of domestic central heating.

CHAPTER 8: ANNA HART

The value of automatic rule induction as a tool for expert knowledge elicitation has been the subject of some controversy. In this chapter, Hart first describes a particular rule induction program (based on the ID3 algorithm) and then provides a detailed case study evaluating its effectiveness as a practical knowledge elicitation tool. She discusses the problems that arise at each stage in the process (e.g., compiling an initial training set, selecting attributes, refining the decision tree) and suggests guidelines for overcoming some of these problems. The final decision tree is compared with the results of an independent interview with the expert. The case study described concerns the procedures carried out by an admissions tutor selecting students for college entrance.

10. REFERENCES

Adams, D. (1979). *The hitchhiker's guide to the galaxy*. London: Pan Books.

Bennett, J. S. (1985). ROGET: A knowledge-based consultant for acquiring the conceptual structure of a diagnostic expert system. *Journal for Automated Reasoning, 1*, 49–74.

Clancey, W. J. (1985). Heuristic classification. *Artificial Intelligence, 27*, 289–350.

Clancey, W. J. (1986). Qualitative student models. *Annual review of computer science, 1*, 381–450.

Clancey, W. J., and Letsinger, R. (1981). NEOMYCIN: Reconfiguring a rule based expert system for applications to teaching. In *Proceedings of the 7th International Joint Conference on Artificial Intelligence*.

Coombs, M., and Alty, J. (1984). Expert systems: An alternative paradigm. *International Journal of Man-Machine Studies, 20*, 21–43.

Elstein, A. S., Shulman, L. S., and Sprafka, S. A. (1978). *Medical problem solving: An analysis of clinical reasoning*. Cambridge, Mass.: Harvard University Press.

Feigenbaum, E. A., and McCorduck, P. (1983). *The fifth generation*. New York: Addison-Wesley.

Hall, R. P., and Kibler, D. F. (1985). Differing methodological perspectives in artificial intelligence research. *AI Magazine*, Fall, 166–178.

Hayes-Roth, F., Waterman, D., and Lenat, D. (Eds.). (1983). *Building expert systems*. Reading, Mass.: Addison-Wesley.

Johnson, Leslie. (1985). The need for competence models in the design of expert systems. *International Journal in Systems Research and Informational Science, 1*, 23–36.

Johnson, Lewis. (1986). Comments made during Intelligent Computer Aided Instruction Workshop, Windermere, UK.

Kidd, A. L. (1985a). The consultative role of an expert system. In P. Johnson and S. Cook (Eds.), *People and computers: Designing the interface*. Cambridge: Cambridge University Press.

Kidd, A. L. (1985b). What do users ask?—Some thoughts on diagnostic advice. In M. Merry (Ed.), *Expert systems 85*. Cambridge: Cambridge University Press.

Kidd, A. L., and Welbank, M. (1984). Knowledge acquisition. In J. Fox (Ed.), *Expert systems*. Infotech State of the Art Report. Maidenhead, England: Pergamon Infotech Ltd.

Marr, D. (1977). Artificial intelligence—A personal view. *Artificial Intelligence, 9*, 37–48.

Michie, D., and Johnston, R. (1985). *The creative computer*. London, England: Pelican.

Mitroff, I. I., and Featheringham, T. R. (1974). On systemic problem solving and the error of the third kind. *Behavioural Science, 19*, 383–393.

Newell, A. (1982). The knowledge level. *Artificial Intelligence, 18*, 87–127.

Nilsson, N. J. (1980). The interplay between experimental and theoretical methods in artificial intelligence. *Cognition and Brain Theory, 4*(1), 69–74.

Norman, D. A. (1986). New views of human information processing: Implications for intelligent decision support. In E. Hollnagel, G. Mancini, and D. D. Woods (Eds.), *Intelligent decision aids*. New York: Springer-Verlag.

Pollack, M. E., Hirschberg, J., and Webber, B. (1982). User participation in the reasoning processes of expert systems. In *Proceedings of the AAAI National Conference*, pp. 358–361.

Prerau, D. S. (1985). Selection of an appropriate domain for an expert system. *AI Magazine*, Summer, 26–30.

Sleeman, D., and Brown, J. S. (Eds.). (1982). *Intelligent tutoring systems*. New York: Academic Press.

Woods, D. D. (1984). Some results on operator performance in emergency events. In D. Whitfield (Ed.), *Ergonomic problems in process operations*. Rugby, England: Institution of Chemical Engineers.

Woods, D. D. (1986). Cognitive technologies: The design of joint human-machine cognitive systems. *AI Magazine*, Winter (6), 86–92.

2

Use of Models in the Interpretation of Verbal Data

JOOST BREUKER and BOB WIELINGA

1. PROBLEMS AND SOLUTIONS IN BUILDING EXPERT SYSTEMS

The experience of building expert systems for a decade has revealed a number of problems and bottlenecks at each stage of the life cycle. Although the evidence is not abundant, because the number of fully operational expert systems is small with respect to the number of systems that have been developed, it appears that *ad hoc* or *post hoc* solutions for problems in early stages can create new and even bigger problems at later stages (McDermott, 1983, 1984): Problems propagate. The fact that few systems ever reach operational maturity is probably indicative of the fact that the art of knowledge engineering is not well established yet. The major problems are listed in the reverse order of their life cycle stages, because problems at later stages are more easily identified.

    1. Expert systems require extensive maintenance. Maintenance problems are not so much attributable to the fact that in many domains of expertise knowledge, insights, and practice may change, but rather that systems are so opaque and unstructured that it is hard to tell where updates and modifications should be applied. Simply adding some new

JOOST BREUKER and BOB WIELINGA • Department of Social Science Informatics, University of Amsterdam, 1016 BS Amsterdam, The Netherlands.

rules may actually decrease performance and lead to unforeseen conflicts (McDermott, 1983b).

2. Once developed and tested, expert systems may fail to be accepted in the intended operational environment, and even fail to satisfy
preset performance criteria. External factors may play a role: E.g., the
performance criteria for expertise may be hard to define, or the user may
not be prepared to accept the system. However, a concomitant and
probably more important factor is that the modality of the system is only
rudimentarily developed. Expertise requires not only problem-solving
competence in a particular domain but also competence to communicate
with the environment—user, client—in order to elicit an intended and
well-specified problem statement (Pollack et al., 1982) and to convey
solutions. Solutions have to be explained, to be justified, or to be transformed into advice, hypotheses, or hints (Miller, 1983). Communicative
expertise to deal with an operational environment is needed to carry the
domain expertise into effect. A practical expert system is not only a
problem-solving system, but it also contains expertise to communicate
about the domain. This expertise is the system's modality. The architecture of the problem solver constrains the modality. Clancey (1983;
Clancey and Letsinger, 1981) showed that adequate explanation facilities
in MYCIN required a complete reconstruction of a system that performed
well as far as diagnosing is concerned. The operational success of R1
(McDermott, 1980) is partially due to the fact that little communicative
competence is required. R1 is a typical autistic problem solver; its de-
scendant XSEL can be viewed as a modality component added to R1
(McDermott, 1983a). Modality involves more than a "man–machine interface"; it embodies communication tasks that require diagnosis and
planning, among other typical problem-solving activities.

3. The best-known problem area in building an expert system is
knowledge acquisition (e.g., Hayes-Roth et al., 1983; Stefik, 1981).
Knowledge acquisition is the process of transforming data on expertise
into an implementation formalism. The problems involved in knowledge acquisition are many. First, there is the problem of selecting and
eliciting data. Most data on expertise in action are not in written form:
Books and other documents contain the theoretical basis or "first principles" (Davis, 1983). This forms the *support knowledge*, which enables the
generation of justifications and other explanations. Support knowledge
may rarely be used even by the expert in solving typical problems (de
Greef and Breuker, 1985). This does not mean that support knowledge is
unimportant for building expert systems—it is indispensable for giving

nontrivial explanations—but that data on expertise can scarcely be found in documents. Not only is there the problem of how to elicit such data on expertise in action, but there is also the fact that elicited verbal data are incomplete and unstructured. Furthermore, these data may be unreliable and contradictory (Breuker, 1981; Ericsson and Simon, 1980, 1984).

Verbal data do not speak for themselves; they have to be interpreted. However, there are no ready-made interpretation frameworks available that satisfy both the requirement that they should map (easily) onto some implementation formalism and that they should structure the data into a coherent description. The major part of this chapter will be concerned with knowledge acquisition and, particularly, with the interpretation problem (cf. Clancey, 1985; Ericsson and Simon, 1984; Welbank, 1983).

4. A fourth problem presents itself right from the start: Is the domain that has been selected apt for the building of an expert system? At what costs and efforts? How much experience and technical support will be required? Solving this feasibility problem requires not only a fair assessment of the complexity of the domain and the available tools, techniques, and know-how at an early stage, but also a choice as to which expertise functions in a domain should be automated. It may be both socially unwise and uneconomical to simply build expert imitators.

Various solutions to these problems have been proposed. The best-known solutions for the knowledge acquisition problem are expert system shells: editors for rule bases with ready-made interpreters (inference engines) (van Melle, 1980). These shells may also support some maintenance functions in providing editing facilities, but more sophisticated maintenance tools have been developed, including conflict resolutions mechanisms, which allow semiautomated maintenance (e.g., TEIRESIAS: Davis, 1977; Davis and Lenat, 1982). Shells may facilitate implementation and (some) information management in dealing with data on expertise, but they also have limitations in the formalisms that are supported. Often, they turn out to be Procrustian beds, where only some form of disabled expertise will fit. In this respect, newly emerging "tool kits" (LOOPS, ART, KEE) provide more degrees of freedom, but the connections between the various formalisms supplied by these tool kits are rather weak. A more integrated approach is provided by KRS (Knowledge Representation System; Steels, 1984). However, tool kits still leave the problem of which formalism adequately represents which type of knowledge and inferencing, and, as a preliminary, how can knowledge and inferencing be identified in the verbal data (cf. Hayes-Roth *et al.*, 1983, p. 153)? There is no knowledge and inferencing typology readily available to facilitate selection and design of architecture. An important exception is ROGET (Bennett, 1985). We will return to this later.

The knowledge acquisition problem can also be attacked from another side: that of the verbal data. The knowledge engineer, who initially plays the role of a student in a new domain, may find it hard to cope with the large amount of data. Advanced word processing and graphic facilities (e.g., Pitman, 1985) can support the process of identifying the relevant domain concepts and terminology and provide some initial means to structure and condense the verbal data—in much the same way as descriptive statistics may do for quantitative data.

Owing to the relatively short experience in building expert systems, it is not surprising that the feasibility problem has scarcely been attacked. Again, ROGET (Bennett, 1985) is such an attempt. It provides feasibility estimates based upon similarity between domain characteristics of MYCIN (diagnosis) and the proposed domain, and upon the experience of the knowledge engineer.

The distinction between problem-solving competence and modality has barely been acknowledged. For instance, Hayes-Roth *et al.* (1983) present a typology of expert systems in which the typical problem-solving tasks and the modality tasks are not distinguished: Data interpretation and instruction are modality tasks rather than proper expert problem-solving tasks.

Expert systems in which modality is an "orthogonal dimension" to expert problem solving is most explicit are intelligent tutoring systems (Sleeman and Brown, 1982). An intelligent tutoring system consists of a "domain expert" and one or more "teaching experts." The teaching experts can be thought of as the modality built around an expert problem-solving system. The teaching expertise includes planning the sequence of subject matter, monitoring and diagnosing student behavior, and providing explanations from various points of view.

2. A METHODOLOGY FOR KNOWLEDGE ACQUISITION

The problems discussed above are widely recognized and call for a careful and systematic approach or methodology. Current practice, however, is not so systematic and is characterized by "rapid prototyping." It is claimed that the "process of building expert systems is inherently experimental" (Hayes-Roth *et al.*, 1983). This suggests at least some degree of trial and error, and discourages the development of a methodology. Knowledge engineering, like any science or engineering activity, is a form of problem solving. Since problem solving itself is the object of study of knowledge engineering, one would expect that principles of effective problem solving would be applied and formalized into a methodology (de Groot, 1970).

From the literature on thinking and problem solving at least two basic heuristics for effective problem solving have emerged. As already asserted by Descartes (see Stefik, 1981), complex problems are easier to solve if partitioned into "nearly decomposable" parts and strategically spaced in time (Simon, 1969). Therefore, a methodology should specify a strategic division of tasks. A second heuristic is that the problem should first be analyzed completely before solution methods are selected and applied. Both heuristics are neglected in rapid prototyping or a bluntly experimental approach. The knowledge engineer performs a wide variety of tasks in a semiparallel fashion; solutions (implementation) are applied before there is a complete analysis of the domain and the functions to be implemented.

In many problem-solving tasks, an adequate problem analysis involves more than just identification of relevant characteristics. In general, a crucial intermediate step is required between identification and the selection of solution methods. Such a step consists of the interpretation of the data into some coherent framework: a model, schema, or canonical form. The larger and more varied the data, the more important such an interpretation model becomes. The functions and nature of interpretation models for knowledge engineering will be discussed in the next section. Here a short overview of the methodology is presented in order to provide the context within which this interpretation—i.e., problem analysis—is performed.

Over the last years we have developed, tried out, and implemented a methodology, called KADS (for Knowledge Acquisition and Documentation Structuring; Breuker and Wielinga, 1985; Wielinga and Breuker, 1984). KADS stands both for the methodology and for the knowledge-based system that supports this methodology. In KADS the problem analysis and the selection of solution methods are decoupled. Analysis, i.e., a major part of the knowledge acquisition activities, precedes the design, implementation, and testing stages. Such decoupling has become standard practice in software engineering. Two major functions in knowledge acquisition can be distinguished:

1. The *elicitation* of data on domain knowledge. At the initial stage of analysis written documentation can and should be used. Because written sources hardly ever contain information on *how*

knowledge is used, other data have to be elicited from experts by interview techniques, and in particular by thinking-aloud procedures. Elicitation techniques differ with respect to the kind of data that can be obtained (as will be shown in Table 2).
2. The *analysis* of verbal data. Analysis is the transformation of data into an interpretative framework. This framework may vary from a weak classification schema to a strong model.

These two major functions are also typical for empirical research in general: Data are collected and interpreted. These functions have a cyclical nature and lead to a further refinement of the interpretative framework. In each cycle new data are collected to test and modify this framework, or model, until it is sufficiently refined, rejected, or replaced by new paradigms (de Groot, 1970). Because in knowledge engineering interpretative frameworks and goals (e.g., functions of the system) cannot be fully specified in advance, the KADS methodology contains three cycles of analysis and elicitation aiming at a description of the basic architecture of a prospective expert system, including modality. Moreover, KADS enables estimates of the feasibility of that system at an early stage of development, and it provides documentation—i.e., a "domain handbook" is created (Grover, 1983). These three refinement cycles are represented by the following stages.

Orientation. The major goals of this stage are the acquisition of a vocabulary of the target domain to identify domain concepts and to communicate with experts, and an assessment of characteristics of the domain, the types of problems and tasks of the expert. These characteristics are used for a selection of potentially applicable interpretation models and for estimating the feasibility of the domain for the construction of an expert system.

Problem Identification. The subtasks here are the uncovering of the structures of the domain concepts, a functional analysis of the prospective expert system, and a task analysis. The structures of domain concepts are the static descriptions of the knowledge involved in the domain. These descriptions have a framelike flavor and consist of hierarchies of classes of objects that are generic to the kind of tasks identified in the task analysis. For instance, in a diagnostic task many of the objects can be classified as evidence, symptom, fault class, etc. Besides the identification of major structures of domain concepts and the typical tasks involved in the expertise, the result of this stage is a definition of the problems the prospective expert system has to solve and the specification of an interpretation model.

TABLE 1. Tasks in KADS Ordered by Topic and by Stage

	Stage		
Topic	Orientation	Problem identification	Problem analysis
Modality	Expert functions identification	Function analysis	User analysis, environment analysis
Feasibility	Domain and task characteristics		Feasibility assessment
Knowledge	Lexicon identification	Structuring of domain concepts	Knowledge base specification[a]
Task/strategy	Task	Task analysis, classification	Process structure definition[a]

[a]These are subtasks of the expert analysis task.

Problem Analysis. This is the most complex stage in knowledge acquisition. An analysis of the user and the operational environment of the prospective system is followed by a very detailed analysis of "expertise in action," i.e., a detailed account of how the problems are solved. This process is described in section 3. The result is a description of the

TABLE 2. Elicitation Techniques, Type of Data that Can Be Validly Obtained, and Stage of Use in KADS Methodology

Technique	Data on	Stage[a] 1	2	3
Focused interview	Factual knowledge	*	*	
	Types of problems			
	Functions of expertise			
Structured interview	Structure of concepts		*	
	Mental models			
	Explanations			
Introspection	Global strategies	*	*	
	Justification			
	Evaluation of solutions			
Thinking aloud	Use of knowledge			*
	Reasoning strategies			
User dialogues	Reasoning strategies			*
	Modality data			
Review of data	Repair of gaps		*	*
	(Re)interpretation of data/analyses			
	Support knowledge			

[a]1 = Orientation stage; 2 = problem identification stage; 3 = problem analysis stage.

basic architecture of the system, and it provides the contraints and data for the design and implementation stages.

The summary description of the tasks involved in the three stages may look more like a heterogeneous collection of topics than like the refinement of a single issue. This is indeed the consequence of taking into account the modality of the system at an early stage of analysis. In Table 1 a summary of tasks, stages, and topics is presented.

The stages are defined in terms of analysis tasks. Parallel to these analysis tasks there are typical elicitation techniques that can be employed at each of these stages. For instance, for the orientation stage, besides written documentation, interviews with experts may provide the required data, while for the problem analysis stage, thinking-aloud protocols are likely to offer the data on expertise in action. Table 2 presents a summary of the type of data that are to be obtained as well as how and when.

3. INTERPRETATION OF DATA ON EXPERTISE

3.1. DOMAINS AND TASKS

In an "experimental" approach the interpretation of data on expertise is considered to be a bottom-up rather than a top-down affair. The domain is unfamiliar to the knowledge engineer, so there is no reason to enter it with strong preconceptions. In the literature there is a strong emphasis on the fact that a typical expert system is based on large amounts of domain-specific knowledge (Feigenbaum, 1979). From such a point of view model-driven interpretation seems a fiction. On the other hand, without preconceptions there is little to be "seen" beyond an overwhelming multitude of individual data. Assembling the pieces of such a puzzle without some model leads to a combinatorial explosion.

In data processing for constructing expert systems the question is not so much whether the approach should be primarily top-down or bottom-up. One would welcome any guiding preconceptions. The question is rather which aspects allow for top-down processing. Aspects that are variable across domains are certainly not suitable for guiding a top-down analysis; aspects that are relatively stable and yet sufficiently specific should be used for model-driven interpretation of data.

Domain-specific knowledge is of course the least suitable candidate. However, thorough studies of expert behavior in several domains show that experts often use systematic problem-solving methods that appear not to be domain-dependent. For example, Pople (1982) claims that an important aspect of clinical reasoning has been overlooked—i.e., the structuring of a diagnostic task on the basis of meta-level knowledge. Stefik (1981) comes to a similar conclusion with respect to planning. Careful analysis of diagnostic systems has revealed task structures that are typical for diagnostic tasks but are relatively domain-independent (cf. Bennet, 1985; Clancey, 1985; Szolovits, 1981). Similarly structured behavior has been observed in thinking-aloud protocols of skilled problem solvers in physics problems (Konst *et al.*, 1983). In summary, expert behavior that is seemingly domain-specific may originate from higher level problem-solving methods, which are well structured and have some degree of domain independence. The task structure therefore appears to be a good point of departure for the design of interpretation models. The structures may vary across types of tasks, but it seems most likely that the number of prototypical tasks is limited (e.g., Guilford, 1967; Hayes-Roth *et al.*, 1983) and relatively independent of domains.

Furthermore, the knowledge that is employed by experts may not be as domain-specific as assumed by Feigenbaum (1979). For instance, while the operations of complex devices can be understood in terms of empirical associations on a surface level, a deeper understanding of a system can be based on conceptual models of underlying principles and causal relations (Bobrow, 1984; Davis, 1983; Gentner and Stevens, 1983). These relations may include abstract notions that hold across a large variety of domains. In our experience over the last three years in analyzing eight widely different domains, a number of concepts have invariably recurred, such as "procedure," "process," "quantificational object" (an object that is individuated by some specific quantitative value for some attribute), and "identificational object" (an object with some nominal value for some attribute). The structure of these abstract concepts is the same across domains, yet their instances are domain-specific.

Such concepts are abstractions of general world knowledge. They include notions such as causality, time, space, and change. These abstract concepts are not part of a particular interpretation model. The abstract concepts are more assumptions of such models than options; such concepts can be knowledge primitives in a knowledge representation tool kit, in the same way as *is-a* (inheritance) and *part-of* concepts are. However, subclasses of such abstract concepts can be both sufficiently specific and typical for a particular type of task to become an ingredient of an interpretation model. For instance, for diagnostic tasks such general concepts as *symptoms, fault class,* and *tests* can classify large amounts of domain-specific concepts into strategic categories. These task-dependent concepts are subclasses of general, abstract concepts: A test is a procedure, a symptom is an identificational object, and so on. In summary, a classification of task structures and of related concepts, which are typical for a type of task, appears to be sufficiently specific and yet domain-independent to serve as a crucial ingredient of interpretation models. We will return to ingredients after discussing at what level these should be described.

3.2. LEVELS OF INTERPRETATION

Interpretation models have several functions. They can be used for communication between expert and knowledge engineer, to check consistency and completeness of elicited data, and, in particular, to facilitate the mapping of these data on expertise on some formalism or structure. The problem is what formalism or structure is to be used.

The most obvious formalisms appear to be implementation formalisms (e.g., rules, frames, inference mechanisms). For instance, a prototype can be viewed as an interpretation model for further knowledge acquisition (cf. Hayes-Roth *et al.*, 1983). However, as suggested above, the implementation formalisms are at too atomic a level to provide some macrostructure to the verbal data. Experts do not express their knowledge and know-how in a rule or framelike formalism, nor are such data easily mapped upon such formalisms. Strategies and inference methods can be abstracted only if such categories as goals, premises, or facts can be read from the data. For knowledge acquisition some special-purpose formalism at an intermediate level is required. This is Newell's (1980) knowledge level, or the "missing level" of Brachman's (1979) analysis of semantic networks. Brachman (1979) identifies primitives for five different levels of representation of static knowledge. These levels are linguistic, conceptual, epistemological, logical, and implementational. These primitives can be extended to the analysis of the verbal data on expertise and the following levels can be distinguished.

Knowledge Identification. This level corresponds with Brachman's linguistic level. At this level individual domain-dependent concepts are identified. This analysis is based mainly on lexical entries (words). Organizing the data by identity provides an important reduction in the data and is a preparation to proper interpretation. Given the large amounts of verbal data, knowledge identification is mainly an information management task. Therefore, automatic support tools like browsers and graphic editors (e.g., CREF; Pitman, 1985) can be very useful. The orientation stage of the KADS methodology is mainly concerned with the identification of knowledge and other objects. At this level the representation is superficial and has not been integrated into a conceptual framework.

Knowledge Conceptualization. At this level individual concepts become integrated according to a number of conceptual primitives. These primitives are abstract, general world concepts, which are the point of departure for classification schemas. The primitives can also include *relations* between concepts. For instance, in KADS *is-a, part-of,* and *causal* structures of relations can be specified, as with many other knowledge representation tools (e.g., KLONE, LOOPS, FLAVORS). The use of these primitives may form a coherent framework, but the structuring principles within this framework are not constrained. The primitives can apply to any domain and task. A good example of the use of primitives at a conceptual level is Schank's conceptual dependency graphs (Schank and Abelson, 1977). Conceptual dependency allows the construction of any structure that represents combinations of events whether they make "sense" or not.

Epistemological Analysis. At the epistemological level the analysis uncovers structural properties of expertise, formalized in an epistemological framework. The epistemological primitives that constitute such a framework are instances of a typology of concepts, knowledge sources, structuring relations, and strategies. This is the missing level in developing expert systems, as indicated in the analyses of Clancey (1983, 1985), Davis (1983), and Bennet (1985).

Logical Analysis. At this level structures are mapped onto formalisms for expressing the knowledge and inferencing. In the KADS methodology the logical analysis is part of the design stage in the development of an expert system.

Implementational Analysis. Here the primitives consist of mechanisms, and they are the ones normally used for describing the implementation of an AI program in terms of matching, testing, slot filling, etc.

Interpretation of verbal data on the epistemological level is a crucial step in the development of an expert system, not only because the gap between data "at the linguistic level" and the implementation level is too wide to be bridged in one step, but also because passing over this level may result in an unstructured and opaque system. Moreover, information may be lost by eclectic use of the data. The question is now what primitives can be proposed at the epistemological level.

3.3. PRIMITIVES OF THE EPISTEMOLOGICAL LEVEL

The epistemological primitives cannot be those proposed by Brachman (1978) and implemented in KLONE because they represent static knowledge; these types of objects and relations are not structurally linked to reasoning strategies. The primitives should enable the specification of relationships between knowledge and strategies. This process of interpretation and specification is illustrated in Figure 1. The specification of the knowledge base can be mapped onto knowledge representation formalisms; that of the structure of the reasoning, on the design of the inference engine.

The strategy-structure-support paradigm advanced by Clancey (1983) as a classification of the knowledge in expert systems is a more adequate candidate. As pointed out by Clancey, different ways to structure knowledge will support different types of strategies. For instance, in CENTAUR (Aikins, 1980) part of the knowledge is structured in a hierarchy of disease prototypes, which allows a top-down refinement strategy as a process (reasoning) structure for this diagnosis task. This hierarchy of disease prototypes is supported by underlying models of the physiological process (pulmonary functions).

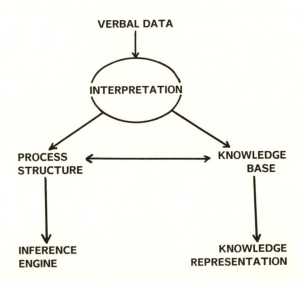

FIGURE 1. Analysis of data for the construction of knowledge-based systems.

Inspired by Clancey's analysis, we have developed five types of primitives from which interpretation models are constructed.

Objects. Objects are the data (input) or conclusions (output) of inference processes. Classes of objects are data, hypotheses, physical objects, processes, actions, plans—i.e., concepts that are instances of abstract knowledge of the world. For each class of tasks typical object (sub)classes can be specified. For instance, typical classes of objects used in a planning task are actions, sequences, and constraints; in diagnostic tasks they are such objects as symptoms, tests, fault classes, and complications.

Knowledge Sources. A knowledge source (KS) is some set of knowledge that infers new objects from given objects. A KS is an "inference association" and is characterized by the kind of inferences that are made (Clancey, 1983). The given objects can be data or conclusions produced by another KS. KSs can be formalized in terms of rules, frame type structures (e.g., Friedland, 1981), or complex processes, as in Hearsay (Lesser *et al.*, 1975). A type of KS that is almost invariably present in an expert system is the classification of data objects in terms of their properties. Transformation KSs transform some structured object into another structured object. Specification is the opposite of classification: Properties are attributed to some object. In composition, objects are assembled, and decomposition is its inverse. More specific KSs may be distinguished—e.g., a causal KS that relates data to causes is a subclass of a specification KS.

Models. Models may be part of the support knowledge or may have a function similar to that of a KS. Types of models include causal models, where processes are causally related; process models, in which relations between events or operations are represented in a conditional rather than a causal way; formal models, based on mathematical theory; empirical models, which specify empirical evidence; and spatial models, which represent spatial relationships between physical objects. As part of support knowledge a model is a basis for justification and allows for relations between reasoning strategies and knowledge structures (Clancey, 1983). Functioning as a KS a model is used by experts for solving unusual cases. Some mental—or qualitative—model of a process is "run" by the expert if the outcomes cannot be foreseen on the basis of "empirical" rules (i.e., experience). Instead of representing models explicitly, most current expert systems use KSs that provide shortcuts in the reasoning steps. Because the structure of models is very complex (cf.

Bobrow, 1984; Gentner and Stevens, 1983) such shortcuts may be warranted for reasons of simplicity of implementation and speed of performance. Analysis of models that experts rely on appears to be indispensable because it facilitates understanding of the expertise and prevents problems in maintaining a system, because the nature of the shortcuts can be documented.

Structures. Not only objects but also KSS can be organized in some structures. The most common structures are hierarchies along some relation, such as sub/superclass, part/whole, general/specific, set/subset. Other organizations are sequences, resemblance groupings around prototypes, and, more loosely, relational networks.

Strategies. A strategy is a plan for invoking problem-solving KSS. In terms of epistemological primitives it controls the use of KSS. In problem solving, strategic planning is required; in expert problem solving, such plans have become more or less fixed in advance. If the strategy is fixed, it is often called a problem-solving method. The typical strategy for solving problems in a particular domain is what novices have to learn, besides the domain-specific knowledge (Mettes *et al.*, 1981). Only in difficult or unusual cases an expert may design or invoke new plans and change strategy, for instance, into reasoning based on "first principles," i.e., on support knowledge (Davis, 1983); the strategy may change from, e.g., a backward chaining strategy into a hypotheticodeductive strategy. Strategies are dependent on the structure of the knowledge base and vice versa (Clancey, 1983). For instance, a top-down refinement strategy can be used for classification if the knowledge base contains a hierarchical structure of distinguishing features (e.g., a decision tree), as implemented in CENTAUR (Aikins, 1980) and in MDX (Chandrasekaran and Mittal, 1983). Implementations of strategies may vary from a fixed order of rule checking or search, the use of specific prewired strategies in the inference engine (e.g., backward chaining), agendas, and specification of metarules (Davis, 1980), to the use of more or less flexible strategic planning components (Stefik, 1981). Other types of strategies, besides backward chaining, top-down refinement, and hypotheticodeductive reasoning, are forward chaining, generate and test, and least commitment, among others.

3.4. INTERPRETATION MODELS

An interpretation model is a generic model of the problem-solving process for a class or prototype of tasks. It looks like a catalog of task-specific ingredients from which selections can be made that appear to match the knowledge structures of the domain. These ingredients are specifications of the primitives discussed before. Prototypical tasks for which interpretation models are developed are (cf. Hayes-Roth *et al.*, 1983, pp. 13–16) as follows:

DIAGNOSIS   Inferring a fault from complaints, symptoms, and other data.

MONITORING   Comparing process parameters with planned values.

PLANNING   Assembling sequences of actions to achieve a goal.

DESIGN   Assembling objects that satisfy constraints.

CONFIGURING   Assembling physical objects that make up a whole.

INFORMATION MANAGEMENT   Interpreting and updating data.

CONVERGENT VALUE FINDING   Finding the unknown value of an object from a description including one or more valued objects.

Many subcategories of typical expert tasks can be distinguished. Diagnosis of malfunctions of physical devices is troubleshooting and differs from diagnosis in general because algorithmic or causal (support) KSs are available. A subcategory of convergent value finding is decision making, where the unknown value is either "accept" or "reject." Another subcategory of convergent value finding is based mainly on formal or semiformal principles, as in solving physics or statistics problems.

It is premature to claim such a list to be exhaustive and elementary. Moreover, within the list of prototypical tasks there are family resemblances. Planning, design, information management, and configuring are more alike than diagnosis, monitoring, and convergent value finding. The former set has as output some composite object that has to satisfy some requirements; the latter produces as a solution a simple (unique) object. Clancey (1985) makes a similar distinction between systems that produce solutions by *synthesis* and those that arrive at a solution by *analysis,* and proposes a subclassification of tasks ("generic operations").

Elementary task types are hard to identify because in practice domain expertise is performed by a composite of often interacting tasks. For instance, in a medical diagnosis task a planning subtask can be distinguished to administer tests for obtaining discriminating evidence with a minimum of costs. The importance and difficulty of such a subtask may be relatively small; therefore, the planning aspect may not be a *typical* component of medical diagnosis. Moreover, such compositions may not be permanent. New tasks may emerge owing to complications. For instance, the tasks in commercial wine making can be summarized as follows (Figure 2; Wielinga and Breuker, 1984): The actual processing of grapes is preceded by planning of the production process and of the constraints for the production process to obtain a specific quality and quantity of wine. During the actual processing of the grapes the wine maker monitors the process on consistency between the planned constraints and the parameter values of intermediate products. If direct negative feedback actions are no longer effective in controlling deviations—e.g., cooling if the temperature gets too high—a diagnosis is performed that may result in an adaptation of the original plan if no other (legal or cost-effective) remedies are available. The relations between the monitoring and diagnosis tasks can be observed only under particular circumstances, and then they are in close interaction. Such a cycle of planning, monitoring, and conditional diagnosis may not be exceptional at all; it may be typical for a wide variety of domains (e.g., in process industries), but also for various modalities (e.g., in coaching; Breuker and de Greef, 1985). It may even be indigenous to any planning and plan execution. In other words, it is likely that the analysis of expertise always involves applying a combination of interpretation models, because the tasks the models stand for are idealized abstractions. There-

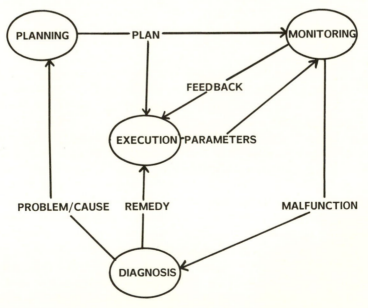

FIGURE 2. Tasks and objects in commercial wine making (cf. Wielinga and Breuker, 1984).

fore, a task classification is required to select interpretation models for a specific domain.

Thus far, interpretation models specify only what classes of knowledge elements are to be identified. The interpretation process requires a number of steps before a process structure is stated and before the elements of this structure are specified in some detail. A process structure—or "conceptual structure" of the task (Bennet, 1985)—specifies what inferences are made and when. This process structure exhibits the basic architecture of the prospective expert system; the specifications provide the more or less refined building blocks. In specifying these building blocks the static relations between concepts are identified. Combined with specifications of knowledge sources, this is the basis for uncovering the inference structure of the expertise. The inference structure describes which inferences can be made by which knowledge sources. The inference structure is a step between the selection, combination, and initial specification of interpretation models and the design of the process structure.

An example of an inference structure is the following: In the design of air-conditioning systems, an initial task is the selection of an appropriate system; the next tasks are the configuring of required components and the design of the piping layout. This system selection task is a typical "convergent find value" task. Which system or combination of systems is chosen is dependent on a decomposition of the total of rooms and floors into zones and calculation of the required heating and cooling loads. This decomposition and the load calculation is based upon the spatial and material data provided by the architect and known—or experimentally obtained—values of the parameters. Therefore, the inference structure can be represented as shown in Figure 3.

However, the inference structure specifies only what inferences are made, but not when they are made and under which conditions. The inference structure does not yet include the strategy specification, which provides the dynamic relations between the components. The diagram in Figure 3 represents the flow of data. It is possible that control follows this flow when there is sufficient decoupling of tasks and subtasks; the inference structure depicts implicitly a forward reasoning strategy. Such a strategy may not be the most effective one. In the example above a backward chaining strategy may reduce the amount of inferencing because in air-conditioning design the solution space is very restricted. However, such a strategy is not supported by the structure of the knowledge. The load calculation is dependent on the zone decomposition and vice versa; an adequate zone decomposition allows for a well-distributed load under varying external conditions. Therefore, a successive refinement strategy appears to be more appropriate, where an initial zone

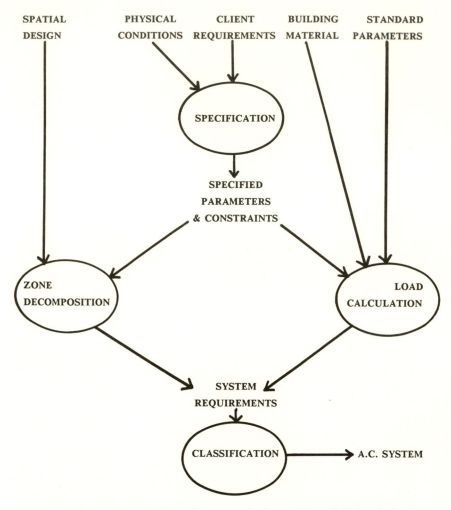

FIGURE 3. Inference structure of system selection in air-conditioning design.

decomposition is made according to some heuristics, followed by a load calculation that can be the base of a more refined zone decomposition. An overview of this process of interpreting the data on expertise is presented in Figure 4.

3.5. USE OF INTERPRETATION MODELS

The use and refinement of interpretation models occurs at the three stages of the KADS methodology. In the orientation stage a task classification is made on the basis of written documentation and one or two focused interviews with the expert(s). An example of such classification is presented in Figure 2 (commercial wine making). The heuristics for task decomposition are not well developed yet (cf. Card *et al.*, 1983). If tasks are performed sequentially, often there are intermediate products; by comparing initial data and products with the typical classes of objects in the various interpretation models, one can deduce the type of task. However, as in the wine-making example, intermediate products may be implicit; they consist of goals the expert assumes to be self-evident. Experience has shown that there is little doubt on what constitutes the major type of task, but subordinate and occasional tasks may be hard to distinguish.

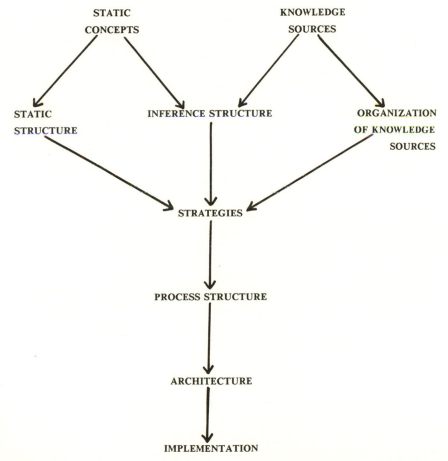

FIGURE 4. Development of a knowledge-based system according to the KADS methodology.

In the problem identification stage the appropriate (assembly of) interpretation model(s) is selected. The object types that are the global "handles" for the inferences provide important initial organizers for the domain-specific knowledge. In a diagnostic domain, for instance, this means that concepts considered to be symptoms, complaints, lab data, etc., are sorted. Concepts may be structured from various points of view. It appears that the structure of concepts that enables inference procedures does not necessarily coincide with order of importance as stated in handbooks or as asserted by the expert; this order rather reflects the theoretical support knowledge, which may often contain concepts that are never used at all in actual performance (de Greef and Breuker, 1985). This structuring of domain concepts is at the same time a check on the appropriateness of the selected interpretation model(s) and may reveal hidden subtasks.

As a transition between this stage and the next, problem analysis, stage, a full-task analysis is performed. The identification of the types of strategies employed leads to a first approximation of the process structure of the expertise. For the identification of strategies there are only few heuristics. The verbal data are almost invariably at too low a level to obtain direct evidence because strategic knowledge is in general not accessible for report. The main source of information is the *order* of use of types of objects (data, hypotheses) and types of inferences, as reported by the expert. From this order a strategy may be abstracted. Furthermore, the order in which the expert elicits data in a (simulated) expert–user interaction can be an important source of information (Clancey, 1983). A realistic order of processing is preserved in thinking-aloud data. Introspective data should be distrusted. We have experienced in a number of domains that what the expert asserts about order of processing may be in full contradiction to actual performance as reflected by thinking-aloud data (Ericsson and Simon, 1979).

A complication is that the expert may not follow one strategy consistently. For instance, physicians may easily abort a hypotheticodeductive strategy if no alternative hypotheses come directly to mind. Such changes of strategy may be interesting from a psychological point of view, but in designing an expert system the knowledge engineer has the freedom—and may prefer—to model a more consistent strategy. Inconsistencies may also indicate in which respect a prospective expert system may support the functioning of an expert.

In the first two stages the data are used in an eclectic way because the data serve specific purposes; in the last stage of analysis of expertise all available (thinking-aloud) data are used in a more systematic way to uncover its structure and fill in its content. In an ideal form this analysis occurs in two steps. First, each statement in the protocol is *identified* in terms of the process model; to each statement or set of statements some identifier or code is attributed that corresponds to some "place" in the interpretation model or process structure. In this way, particularly, the KSS become further specified with detailed, but incoherent and potentially conflicting, information. One may choose some coding formats and translate statements into pseudorules, for instance, in order to facilitate the second step: further interpretation. Further interpretation consists of (1) grouping facts in such a way that it may result in further decomposition of some KS; (2) abstracting knowledge from specific information in the protocol according to the structure of concepts—or "bottom-up": i.e., inducing common features; (3) checking consistency between facts.

This last cycle of lower-level interpretation and further specification of the process model is performed by "eye" rather than from explicit machine support, because detailed heuristics to guide the knowledge engineer in interpreting the data are still under development. The process model consists of flow diagrams of objects and KS (i.e., the inference structure), strategy specifications (cf. Figure 4), structures of objects (*part-of, is-a,* etc., hierarchies), and specifications of KS (e.g., rule sets). When translated into implementation formalisms this document forms the functional specification of the prospective system. Important help in monitoring this emergence of the basic architecture of the system can be obtained from the expert by having him review the interpretations. This function is similar to the expert evaluating the performance of a prototype. Advantages are that a process model may be much more transparent than a flat rule base, that deficiencies in system behavior are often hard to identify, and that adapting this model is much less costly than debugging or rebuilding a prototype system.

However, the interpretation process is not foolproof. Each stage implies a check on the completeness and correctness of a previous stage. While not excluding debugging completely, these checks prevent deep backtracking (cf. Hayes-Roth *et al.*, 1983, Chap. 4.). Backtracking in KADS has a limited scope and, therefore, limited costs. The result of this interpretation process is a rather fine-grained description of the basic architecture of the prospective system, consisting of the global flow of data and of control; the main structuring of the domain concepts; a knowledge base which is partitioned according to the types of inference that are supported, and which contains as many facts as the data provide information about; and a description of the required inference engine.

The analysis of the modality of the system follows another track, as is indicated by Table 1. If the required modality of the system is complex, its structure has to be acquired by a similar process of data collecting and data interpretation. Data that are particularly suitable for a specification of the modality are user-expert dialogues and mock-up sessions, during which expert and user communicate via terminals, and the thinking-aloud protocols of both of them are elicited. In the last stage, the modality tasks have to be integrated with the problem-solving architecture of the prospective system.

3.6. SUPPORTING KNOWLEDGE ACQUISITION: KADS AND ROGET

The KADS methodology is to a large extent formalized and implemented in a knowledge-based system. The KADS system is an interactive support tool for knowledge acquisition and provides a number of functions like guidance by planning tasks for the knowledge engineer, support at data interpretation, and feasibility estimation, and a number of information management functions, like on-line information retrieval, consistency checking, and generation of documentation and of parts of the prospective expert system.

The pilot version of the KADS system is implemented in Prolog. In the centre of KADS is a semantic network based on KLONE (Brachman, 1978). This network contains knowledge about the analysis tasks, a number of domain-independent concepts, and the domain knowledge. The system has a simple inference machine to drive production rules for feasibility assessment, consistency checking, elicitation planning, and interpretation heuristics. The rules are part of the network and allow (semi) object-oriented processing. The analysis component controls the interactive analysis of the domain by instantiating and updating knowledge structures that represent the analysis task. The KADS system has a graphic editor and browser enabling the inspection and modification of both the domain-independent knowledge base and the specific domain data—e.g., the lexicon, the structures of concepts, and the process structure (for a more detailed description of the KADS system see Breuker and Wielinga, 1985).

The ROGET system (Bennet, 1985) for acquiring the conceptual (= process) structure of expertise sustains a refinement process similar to that of the KADS system. An initial interpretation model or "skeletal conceptual structure" is selected representing the type of task and expectations about the kinds of knowledge objects in the domain. ROGET contains heuristics to estimate the feasibility of constructing an expert system. It also can propose particular tasks in the process structure to be pruned, if the prospective system is becoming too complex with respect to the experience the user has in building expert systems. Although it is not explicitly mentioned, ROGET supports an analysis at the epistemological level. Like XPLAIN (Swartout, 1981), but unlike KADS, ROGET constructs a prototype expert system as a result of this refinement process in an EMYCIN shell (van Melle, 1980). This also entails some limitations of ROGET. The system only supports diagnostics tasks and MYCIN-like reasoning structures.

These limitations are not of a principal nature. ROGET can be extended to cover other types of tasks—in particular, planning—and can be equipped with an implementation environment that will allow architectures other than the classical MYCIN one. Similarly, KADS will be extended with semiautomated tools for building expert systems to support the design and implementation stages.

An important difference between the approach advocated here and ROGET is the use and nature of data. In ROGET the data consist of direct answers from the user about concepts and facts of the domain. The system branches into more specific questions generated on the basis of the selected initial conceptual structure and answers to previous questions. These questions are answered by the knowledge engineer, but the domain-specific questions may also be used to elicit information from the expert in direct interaction with the system (cf. TEIRESIAS; Davis and Lenat, 1982). To answer such specific questions the required knowledge should be easily identifiable and unambiguous. KADS, however, also supports the elicitation and identification of knowledge. The interactions concerning domain-specific knowledge are mediated via data that are obtained from the expert by a wide variety of elicitation techniques.

A second difference between KADS and ROGET is that in the latter the refinement strategy follows a depth-first course after selection of the interpretation model; in KADS the breadth-first refinement is the consequence of broadening the scope of the analysis so as to include the modality of the system. These differences are more like differences in focus. ROGET is modeled after the analysis of existing expert systems, in particular the MYCIN family; KADS is patterned after the analysis of human problem solving and expert behavior. Automatization of expertise requires understanding of both human and automated reasoning. Both approaches and know-how are complementary.

4. CONCLUDING REMARKS

Is the KADS methodology a remedy against the problems and bottlenecks in constructing expert systems, as explained in the first section of this chapter? The methodology has been applied to analyse expertise in a wide variety of domains, such as management of planning data bases (Breuker & Wielinga, 1984a), commercial wine making (Wielinga and Breuker, 1984), VLSI design, exhibition planning (Starzun *et al.*, 1984a), air-conditioning design (Starzun *et al.*, 1984b), commercial loans assessment, and consultancy for statistical testing (de Greef and Breuker, 1985). These experiences have shown that the method is effective and that it can be employed even by novice knowledge engineers.

These experiences are not yet conclusive for various reasons. The first reason is that in only a few cases (4) have actual systems been constructed; none of these is operational yet. Therefore, claims on improvement of maintainability and operational functionality cannot be substantiated by direct empirical evidence. A second reason is that in only a few studies comparisons could be made with traditional approaches. In one case (Breuker and Wielinga, 1984b) KADS was clearly superior to rapid prototyping. The amount of data required and the analysis effort were less, and the quality of results in terms of modularity, transparency, and completeness was clearly better. At least with respect to problems in knowledge acquisition—the major bottleneck in expert system development—there is evidence that the KADS methodology is effective.

In the majority of these empirical studies the descriptions of the architecture of prospective systems appear to be more transparent and articulate than those reported in the literature for similar tasks. Furthermore, such structures provide a good insight into the potential bottlenecks in constructing the system, so that qualified estimates of its feasibility can be based on it, as in ROGET. In this respect, however, empirical evidence is particularly lacking. In summary, KADS appears to be an effective support in solving problems in knowledge acquisition—as it is intended to do—which may have beneficial effects with solving some of the other problem areas: feasibility estimates, operational performance and acceptance, and maintainability.

5. GUIDELINES SUMMARY

The KADS methodology is based upon a number of principles, which are derived from methodologies in various disciplines (psychology, software engineering) and experiences in building expert systems. We think that these principles are more important than the specific way we have expressed them in the KADS methodology. The principles can be viewed as epitomizing the support knowledge of KADS, and they can be read as high-level guidelines in knowledge analysis for expert systems. The principles can be stated as follows:

- The knowledge and expertise should be analyzed before design and implementation starts; i.e., the major efforts in knowledge acquisition should occur before an implementation formalism is chosen. Benefits are the following: (1) Feasibility of the domain for constructing an expert system can be assessed with few costs and at an early time. (2) The construction or choice of knowledge representation and inference formalisms can be motivated. (3) The analysis provides a detailed overview of the architecture of the prospective system. This overview permits refinement from newly acquired data. If this architecture appears to be inappropriate, major revisions are less costly than if the knowledge acquisition proceeds mainly by prototype implementation.
- Preferably, the analysis should be model-driven as early as possible. Models of expert problem solving not only enable (at least, facilitate) the analysis of data but also provide references to known implementation solutions (cf. ROGET; Bennett, 1985).
- To bridge the gap between verbal data on expertise and implementation a model of expert problem solving should be expressed at the epistemological (knowledge) level (Clancey, 1985).
- The analysis should include the functionality of the prospective system; i.e., data on the environment and users should be collected and analyzed. These data are used for defining the communication tasks—modality—of the system.
- The analysis should proceed, preferably, in an incremental way. Because there is a wide variety of topics, such as tasks, functions, knowledge, that are not unrelated, the analysis should be breadth-first and cyclical to allow successive refinement and inclusion of results of analysis of related topics.
- New data should be elicited only when previously collected data have been analyzed; i.e., elicitation and analysis should alternate. This should both keep the data manageable and lead to more specific topics for, and methods of, elicitation (Breuker and Wielinga, 1984b).
- Collected data and interpretations should be documented. On-line documentation of the analysis is a *conditio sine qua non* for teamwork. The *Domain Handbook* (Grover, 1983) is also an excellent guide for system maintenance.

ACKNOWLEDGMENT. The research reported was funded in part by the ESPRIT program of the European Community by contract 12/3.2, "Methodology for the Design of Knowledge-Based Systems."

6. REFERENCES

Aikins, J. S. (1980). Prototypes and production rules: A knowledge representation for computer consultations. Report HPP-80-17. Stanford, Calif.: Stanford University.

Bennett, J. S. (1985). ROGET: A knowledge-based consultant for acquiring the conceptual structure of a diagnostic expert system. *Journal for Automated Reasoning, 1,* 49–74.

Bobrow, D. (Ed.). (1984). Special issue on qualitative reasoning. *Artificial Intelligence, 24,* 1–3. Also as: D. Bobrow (Ed.). (1984). *Qualitative reasoning about physical systems.* Amsterdam: North-Holland, and Cambridge, Mass.: M.I.T. Press.

Brachman, R. J. (1978). *A structural paradigm for representing knowledge.* BBN Technical Report. Cambridge, Mass.: Bolt Beranek and Newman.

Brachman, R. J. (1979). On the epistemological status of semantic networks. In N. V. Findler (Ed.), *Associative networks.* New York: Academic Press.

Breuker, J. A. (1981). *Availability of knowledge.* Doctoral dissertation, COWO 81-JB, University of Amsterdam.

Breuker, J. A., and de Greef, P. (1985). *Functional specification of teaching and coaching strategies for EUROHELP.* Report 4.2., ESPRIT Project 280. Amsterdam: University of Amsterdam.

Breuker, J. A., and Wielinga, B. J. (1984a). *Initial analysis for knowledge based systems: An example.* Report 1.3a, ESPRIT Project 12. Amsterdam: University of Amsterdam.

Breuker, J. A., and Wielinga, B. J. (1984b). *Overview of case studies in knowledge acquisition.* Report 1.8, ESPRIT Project 12. Amsterdam: University of Amsterdam.

Breuker, J. A., and Wielinga, B. J. (1985). KADS: Structured knowledge acquisition for expert systems. *Proceedings of Fifth International Workshop on Expert Systems and Their Applications,* Avignon, France.

Card, S. K., Moran, T. P., and Newell, A. (1983). *The psychology of human-computer interaction.* Hillsdale, N.J.: Erlbaum.

Chandrasekaran, B., and Mittal, S. (1983). Deep versus compiled knowledge approaches to diagnostic problem solving. *International Journal of Man-Machine Studies, 19,* 425–436.

Clancey, W. J. (1983). The epistemology of rule-based expert systems: A framework for explanation. *Artificial Intelligence, 20,* 215–251.

Clancey, W. J. (1985). Heuristic classification. *Artificial Intelligence, 27,* 289–350.

Clancey, W. J., and Letsinger, R. (1981). NEOMYCIN: Reconfiguring a rule based expert system for applications to teaching. *Proceedings of the 7th International Joint Conference on Artificial Intelligence.*

Davis, R. (1977). Interactive transfer of expertise: Acquisition of new inference rules. *Proceedings of the 5th International Joint Conference on Artificial Intelligence.*

Davis, R. (1980). Meta-rules: Reasoning about control. *Artificial Intelligence, 15,* 179–222.

Davis, R. (1983). Reasoning from first principles in electronic trouble-shooting. *International Journal of Man-Machine Studies, 19,* 403–423.

Davis, R., and Lenat, D. (1982). *Knowledge based systems in artificial intelligence.* New York: McGraw-Hill, 1982.

de Greef, P., and Breuker, J. A. (1985). A case study in structured knowledge acquisition. *Proceedings of the 9th International Joint Conference on Artificial Intelligence.*

de Groot, A. D. (1970). *Methodology.* The Hague: Mouton.

Ericsson, K. A., and Simon, H. A. (1980). Verbal reports as data. *Psychological Review, 87,* 215–251.

Ericsson, K. A., and Simon, H. A. (1984). *Protocol analysis, verbal reports as data.* Cambridge, Mass.: M.I.T. Press.

Feigenbaum, E. A. (1979). Themes and case studies of knowledge engineering. In D. Michie (Ed.), *Expert systems in the micro-electronic age.* Edinburgh: Edinburgh University Press.

Friedland, P. (1981). Acquisition of procedural knowledge from domain experts. *Proceedings of the 7th International Joint Conference on Artificial Intelligence.*

Gentner, D., and Stevens, A. (Eds.). (1983). *Mental models.* Hillsdale, N.J.: Erlbaum.

Grover, M. D. (1983). A pragmatic knowledge acquisition methodology. *Proceedings of the 8th International Joint Conference on Artificial Intelligence.*

Guilford, J. P. (1967). *The nature of human intelligence.* New York: Academic Press.

Hayes-Roth, F., Waterman, D. A., and Lenat, D. B. (Eds.). (1983). *Building expert systems.* Reading, Mass.: Addison-Wesley.

Konst, L., Wielinga, B. J., Elshout, J. J., and Jansweijer, W. N. (1983). Semi-automated analysis of protocols from novices and experts solving physics problems. *Proceedings of the 8th International Joint Conference on Artificial Intelligence.*

Lesser, V. R., Fennell, R. D., Erman, L. D., and Reddy, D. R. (1975). Organization of HEARSAY II speech understanding system. *IEEE Transactions on Acoustics, Speech, and Signal Processing, 23,* 11–24.

McDermott, J. (1980). R1: The formative years. *AI Magazine, 2,* 21–29.

McDermott, J. (1983a). Extracting knowledge from expert systems. *Proceedings of the 8th International Joint Conference on Artificial Intelligence,* pp. 100–107.

McDermott, J. (1983b). *Building expert systems.* CMU report. Carnegie-Mellon University, Pittsburgh.

Mettes, C. T., Pilot, A., and Roosink, H. J. (1981). Linking factual and procedural knowledge in solving science problems: A case study in a thermodynamics course. *Instructional Science, 10,* 333–361.

Miller, P. L. (1983). Medical plan analysis by computer. *MEDINFO 83,* pp. 593–599.

Newell, A. (1980). Physical symbol systems. *Cognitive Science, 4,* 135–183.

Pitman, K. M. (1985). *CREF, an editing facility for managing structured text.* HCRL Tech. Report 14. The Open University, Milton Keynes, U.K.

Pollack, M., Hirschberg, J., and Webber, B. (1982, August). User participation in the reasoning processes of expert systems. *Proceedings of the AAAI-82 National Conference on Artificial Intelligence,* Pittsburgh, pp. 358–361 (Longer version: University of Pennsylvania Technical Report MS-CIS-82-9, 1982).

Pople, H. E. (1981). Heuristic methods for imposing structure on ill structured problems: The structuring of medical diagnosis. In P. Szolovits (Ed.), *Artificial intelligence in medicine.* Boulder, Colo.: Westview Press.

Schank and Abelson (1975). *Scripts, Plans, Goals, and Understanding.* Hillsdale, N.J.: Erlbaum.

Simon, H. A. (1969). The science of design and the architecture of complexity. In H. A. Simon (Ed.), *Sciences of the artificial.* Cambridge, Mass.: M.I.T. Press.

Sleeman, D., and Brown, J. S. (Eds.). (1982). *Intelligent tutoring systems.* New York: Academic Press.

Starzun, S., *et al.* (1984a). *A KADS case study in exhibition planning (APE).* Report 1.7, ESPRIT Project 304/12. London: Knowledge Based Systems Centre, Polytechnic of the South Bank.

Starzun, S., *et al.* (1984b). *A KADS case study in air conditioning design (ACE).* Report 1.6, ESPRIT Project 304/12. London: Knowledge Based Systems Centre, Polytechnic of the South Bank.

Steels, L. (1984). Design requirements for knowledge representation systems. In J. Laubsch (Ed.), *Proceedings of GWAI-83.* Berlin: Springer-Verlag.

Stefik, M. (1981). Planning with constraints (MOLGEN: Part 1). *Artificial Intelligence, 16,* 111–140.

Swartout, W. R. (1981). *Producing explanations and justifications of expert.* Doctoral dissertation, Massachusetts Institute of Technology.

Szolovits, P. (Ed.). (1981). *Artificial intelligence in medicine.* Boulder, Colo: Westview Press.

van Melle, W. (1980). *System aids in constructing consultation programs.* Ann Arbor, Mich.: UMI Research Press.

Welbank, M. A. (1983). *A review of knowledge acquisition techniques for expert systems.* Ipswich: Martelsham Consultancy Service.

Wielinga, B. J., and Breuker, J. A. (1984). Interpretation models for knowledge acquisition. In T. O'Shea (Ed.), *Advances in artificial intelligence.* Amsterdam: North-Holland.

3

Knowledge Acquisition by Analysis of Verbatim Protocols

BENJAMIN KUIPERS and JEROME P. KASSIRER

1. INTRODUCTION

How does an expert physician reason about the mechanisms of the body? We are exploring the hypothesis that the physician has a cognitive "causal model" of the patient: a description of the mechanisms of the human body and how they influence each other. This causal model, incorporating the expert's knowledge of anatomy and physiology, can be used to simulate the normal working of the body, its pathological behavior in a diseased state, and the idiosyncracies that characterize a particular patient. The causal model supports the expert performance of the physician by simulating the possible courses of the patient's disease and treatment, by serving as a coherency criterion on hypotheses about the patient's state, and by providing a common framework for explanations and discussion among physicians.

If intelligent computer programs are to provide genuinely expert levels of performance in medicine, they must incorporate some sort of causal model, both to support expert problem-solving and to provide an acceptable interface with physicians. Research in artificial intelligence recently has begun to address the problems of causal reasoning in diag-

BENJAMIN KUIPERS • Department of Computer Sciences, University of Texas at Austin, Austin, Texas 78712.   JEROME P. KASSIRER • Department of Medicine, Tufts University School of Medicine, Boston, Massachusetts 02111. This is an updated version of an article that originally appeared in *Cognitive Science*, 8, 363–385, 1984. Reprinted by permission.

nosis, explanation, and troubleshooting, focusing primarily on problems in electronics, in simple physics, and in medicine (de Kleer, 1977, 1979; de Kleer and Brown, 1984; Forbus, 1981, 1984; Kuipers, 1982, 1984; Patil, 1981; Pople, 1982). This work has been important in identifying computational constraints on knowledge representations for causal reasoning, but in most cases it has been only loosely constrained by empirical study of the way human experts actually solve problems. Cognitive scientists such as Chi *et al.* (1982) and Larkin *et al.* (1980) have studied the ways that experts and novices formulate and solve word problems in physics, but without specifying the knowledge representations and implementing working computer simulations. We believe that it is important to unify these two approaches, to develop techniques for designing knowledge representations constrained by empirical observations. Our goal in this chapter is to demonstrate a method we have used successfully to analyze physician behavior in detail and to derive critical properties of the knowledge representation. Taking these empirical constraints along with computational constraints on knowledge representations has allowed us to create a working program that simulates the reasoning processes of the physician.

To understand in detail how a human expert reasons about causal relationships is of pragmatic benefit to the designers of expert systems for two reasons. First, if the causal model is to support clear explanations and be an important part of the interface between expert program and expert human, then its structure should be very similar to that used by the human. Second, we are just learning how to represent causal knowledge so that programs can manipulate it effectively. We are likely to be able to extract valuable clues about the representation and manipulation of causal knowledge, at all levels of detail, by looking carefully at the behavior of expert humans.

The construction of genuinely expert knowledge-based systems requires several different methods of knowledge acquisition. Davis (1982) describes methods for supporting domain experts in providing new knowledge and debugging existing knowledge in a large rule-based system. However, his approach is limited to operating within the knowledge representation chosen by the system designers. It is also important to develop methods for studying experts to determine the *representation* for the knowledge base, even before attempting to capture large quantities of domain knowledge. The research presented here addresses that problem: of examining the behavior of individual experts to determine the representation of their knowledge, and the collection of domain concepts that should be considered fundamental.

2. DESIGN OF THE EXPERIMENT

Most existing research on clinical cognition has used experimental methods designed to gather data that could be combined across many subjects and analyzed using existing statistical techniques (e.g., de Dombal *et al.*, 1972; Rimoldi, 1961). These methods are appropriate to the scientific fields (e.g., biomedicine) where competing hypotheses exist to explain the existing data, and the goal of the scientist is to refute one or the other hypothesis with a reliable, repeatable experiment. In artificial intelligence, however, we typically have no detailed hypotheses adequate to explain even those facts about knowledge representations that we already know. We need a methodology of discovery, to determine constraints from human behavior that can help us develop adequate hypotheses about the structure of knowledge representations. There are two basic questions we want to answer about the behavior of an unknown knowledge representation that will aid in determining its structure: (1) What states of knowledge can be expressed? (2) What inferences can take place?

A methodology of discovery appropriate to the undoubted complexity of human knowledge requires rich data about individuals rather than easily analyzed data about a population. Individual variation is such a striking feature of human cognition that any attempt to average data across a population is certain to mask the true structure of the knowledge. As Newell and Simon (1972) point out, only the full complexity of verbal behavior, as captured in a verbatim transcript, can do justice to the complexity of the knowledge representation. Therefore, in order to study the representation of causal knowledge in physicians, we decided to analyze verbatim transcripts of a small number of physicians solving problems using their causal knowledge.

The fidelity of the setting is another issue in studying problem-solving behavior. Experimental designs have ranged from recording the responses of subjects to data on a fixed set of cards (Rimoldi, 1961), to collecting verbatim transcripts of the responses a physician gives to a predigested case description (Kassirer and Gorry, 1978), to videotaping physician interactions with actors trained to simulate patients (Elstein *et al.*, 1978). On the one hand, it is important to allow the experimental design to reflect a richness of response sufficient to illuminate the complex structure of knowledge representations. On the other hand, the difficulty and cost of collecting and analyzing the data is an important consideration.

After analyzing the alternate methods (Kassirer, Kuipers, and Gorry, 1982), we concluded that an interview based on a detailed printed description of a patient, and resulting in a verbatim transcript, was both more cost-effective and more powerful than the simulated patient encounter to explore the knowledge representation. Note that problem solving from predigested clinical data is a natural activity for physicians, particularly during residency but also in consultations and other conferences among physicians. While this activity is clearly distinct from the natural patient encounter, we expect that the problem-solving techniques and the nature of the medical knowledge used are very similar.

We designed an interview as a "thinking-aloud" experiment, in which the subject is asked to report as much as possible of what he thinks about as he solves a problem. The interviewer intervenes only with nondirective reminders to keep thinking aloud. This type of experiment is particularly sensitive to the natural control structure of the subject's problem-solving method. The experimenter can usually conclude that information reported was actually in the subject's focus of attention at the time, but of course much of what the subject had in mind necessarily goes unreported. Thus, it is not possible to draw direct conclusions about the limits of the subject's knowledge.

We have complemented the thinking-aloud experiment with a "cross-examination" experiment, in which the experimenter asks probing questions about the subject's knowledge of particular topics. The cross-examination interview is not sensitive to the natural control structure of the problem-solving method but is much more effective for determining the limits of the knowledge represented, particularly in highly articulate subjects such as physicians. When a subject is being asked to solve only a single problem, the two methods can be combined in an interview that begins with a thinking-aloud segment and ends with a cross-examination.

In a recent survey (Kassirer et al., 1982), we reviewed the methodologies for investigating clinical cognition and described some of the pitfalls and promise of the analysis of verbatim transcripts of physicians solving realistic medical problems. Although the work of Elstein et al. (1978) is important and path-breaking, we criticized it for its reliance on retrospective reflections of physicians when viewing videotapes of their own behavior (Kassirer et al., 1982). In an extensive review, Nisbett and Wilson (1977) show that a subject has no privileged knowledge of the factors that influence his behavior. Ericsson and Simon (1980) develop a model of the verbalization process and use it to clarify and refine Nisbett and Wilson's conclusion. They conclude that a subject's statement of what is currently in his focus of attention is unlikely to be in error, but that his commonsense theory of his own cognitive processes has no particular privileged status. Newell and Simon (1972) provide a clear description of their use of this distinction:

> There is much confusion in psychology about how to deal with verbal data. It is worth emphasizing that we are not treating these protocols as introspections. Actually, there are very few introspective utterances in them. An example does occur at B87:
>
> B86: Exp: *What are you thinking now?*
> B87: *I was just trying to think over what I was just—*
>
> We treat this utterance only for the evidence it gives of the subject's knowledge or operation—in this case, essentially no evidence. The protocol is a record of the subject's ongoing behavior, and an utterance at time *t* is taken to indicate knowledge or operation at time *t*. Retrospective accounts leave much more opportunity for the subject to mix current knowledge with past knowledge, making reliable inference from the protocol difficult. Nor, in the thinking-aloud protocol, is the subject asked to theorize about his own behavior—only to report the information and intentions that are within his current sphere of conscious awareness. All theorizing about the causes and consequences of the subject's knowledge state is carried out and validated by the experimenters, not by the subject. (p. 184)

The expert physician, with many years of experience, has so "compiled" his knowledge that a long chain of inference is likely to be reduced to a single association. This feature can make it difficult for an expert to verbalize information that he actually uses in solving a problem. Faced with a difficult problem, the apprentice fails to solve it at all, the journeyman solves it after long effort, and the master sees the answer immediately. Clearly, although the master has the knowledge we want to study, the journeyman will be much easier to study by our methods. The attempts of the apprentice may also be illuminating, particularly in clarifying the relationship between textbook learning and clinical experience. Accordingly, we selected subjects at three widely spaced levels of expertise: medical school faculty members (the masters), second-year residents (the journeymen), and fourth-year medical students (the apprentices). The scope of this paper, however, only permits us to discuss results from a single subject (a journeyman).

The material for the interview consisted of a slightly atypical case of a kidney disorder called the *nephrotic syndrome,* presented as a case summary on a single sheet of paper. In the nephrotic syndrome, a patient retains salt and water and suffers swelling (*edema*) of the face and legs; the swelling is an important diagnostic finding. Because of a self-induced low-salt diet, this particular patient experienced no swelling, though all other signs and laboratory results allowed an unambiguous diagnosis to be made. The interview began with a thinking-aloud section in which the subject made and discussed the diagnosis, and concluded with a cross-examination section to probe for explanations of particular issues. The atypical case allowed us to compare three different causal models in the same subject: the model of salt and water handling by the healthy kidney, the pathophysiology of the nephrotic syndrome, and the idiosyncracies of the particular patient.

3. THE NEPHROTIC SYNDROME

The nephrotic syndrome case was selected to investigate causal reasoning about equilibrium processes, which are central to physiological mechanisms. Two important equilibrium processes are disturbed in the nephrotic syndrome: the transfer of salt and water across capillary walls (the *Starling equilibrium*) and the transfer of salt and water from the plasma into the urine. The Starling equilibrium determines the flow of water between the plasma and the tissues (the spaces between the cells), according to the balance of competing *hydrostatic pressure* and *oncotic pressure* in the plasma and in the tissues. The second important equilibrium, also controlled by the kidney, determines the total amount of salt and water in the body. Under normal circumstances, if the body contains too much salt and water, the kidney excretes more of each into the urine; if there is too little, it cuts back on excretion.

In the nephrotic syndrome, both of these equilibria are shifted to new stable points, changing the quantity of salt and water in the body and causing problems for the patient. The basic cause of nephrotic syndrome is that the diseased kidney excretes protein that it was supposed to retain, and consequently plasma proteins (particularly albumin) are depleted. The amount of protein in the plasma determines its oncotic pressure and hence is an important factor in the Starling equilibrium. With less protein in the blood, the Starling equilibrium shifts, moving some water from the plasma into the tissues. This movement of extra water into the tissues in itself usually causes no clinical manifestations. However, the shift of water to the tissues leaves the plasma volume low, so the kidney starts to retain water rather than allowing it to be excreted in the urine. The Starling equilibrium, of course, continues to shift much of this additional fluid into the tissues, and substantial edema develops. From the patient's point of view, this accumulation can produce as much as 50 pounds of extra water in the legs and abdomen. To understand the mechanism of edema in nephrotic syndrome requires an understanding of both equilibria and their interaction (Figure 1).

Retention of salt by the kidney is central to the mechanism whereby

kidney "leaks" protein into the urine
⇓
low serum protein
⇓
fluid flow into tissues
⇓
low plasma volume
⇓
sodium retention by the kidney
⇓
water retention (isotonic) by the kidney
⇓
edema

FIGURE 1. A diagrammatic representation of the causal relations in nephrotic syndrome.

the kidney retains water. In response to a contraction of plasma volume, the kidney's primary response is to retain salt. Salt retention, in turn, is what causes water retention. The particular patient whose history formed the basis of the experiment had selected a low-salt diet, so the kidney was unable to retain much salt or water, and the edema was consequently much less than a physician would expect, based on the severe decrease in blood proteins. Our subjects all understood this association, but probes of the mechanism by which it works revealed limits to the subjects' knowledge.

Typical of these limits is the treatment of the physical forces, *osmotic pressure* and *oncotic pressure*. A good explanation of nephrotic syndrome must refer to both kinds of pressure, but they can be treated as "black boxes." On the other hand, the mechanisms behind these forces cannot be adequately explained using a linearized "A causes B" explanation. And in fact, although the more expert physicians used the concepts of osmotic and oncotic pressure correctly, subjects at all levels of expertise gave very weak explanations of how they are caused.

4. ANALYSIS OF THE TRANSCRIPT

The raw data produced by the experiment is a verbatim transcript of the subject's explanation of various aspects of the nephrotic syndrome in general and of this case in particular. As it is transcribed, the transcript is broken into short lines that correspond roughly to meaningful phrases in the explanation (see Table 1). How this task is accomplished is not critical, but the format eases the burden of later analysis. Out of the transcript as a whole, selections are made of excerpts in which the subject appears to be concentrating on the explanation and presenting his medical knowledge, rather than expressing an opinion about his own mental processes.

TABLE 1. A Second-Year Resident Explains How Loss of Protein from the Blood Causes Edema in Nephrotic Syndrome[a]

L162	A: When there is a very low *albumin* in the serum,
L163	there are two forces which cause edema in my thinking—
L164	the hydrostatic and oncotic forces
L165	and we have actually opposed forces,
L166	forces [. . .break. . .] formation is secondary to
L167	the hydrostatic force of the blood going through the capillaries
L168	and causing the transudation of *fluid*
L169	as well as the osmotic force within the blood vessels,
L170	that is secondary to the *proteins* in the plasma
L171	which tend to draw *fluid*
L172	from the interstitial spaces into the blood vessels
L173	and also there is the forces in the extracellular space.
L174	There are certain *proteins* which tend to pull *water*
L175	out of the blood vessels
L176	and there is a hydrostatic force I believe also in the interstitial spaces
L177	which can counteract the force of the fluid
L178	coming out from within the vessels
L179	and if you have a very low albumin in the serum,
L180	there will be a decreased osmotic pressure
L181	and make it easier for the *fluid* to go out into the interstitial spaces.

Substances
    Protein (L162, 170, 174, 179)
    Fluid (L168, 171, 174, 181)

[a]The first stage in the analysis consists of identifying and classifying the phrases in the excerpt referring to *substances*. Similar analyses identify references to locations, concentrations, forces, and flow rates (cf. Table 2).

The analysis of an excerpt takes place in two stages: (1) Identify the objects and relations in the domain that the subject is referring to, as distinct from the wording used to refer to them. (2) Identify the causal relationships that are described in the segment. Table 1 presents an excerpt in which the subject, a second-year resident in internal medicine, is explaining (correctly) the mechanism by which the loss of protein from the blood results in edema in nephrotic syndrome. A quick reading of the excerpt shows that the physician is framing his explanation in terms of *substances* in *locations*, causing *forces* that result in *flows*. By attempting to classify each referring phrase in the extract into one of these categories, we can test whether our initial hypothesis about the framework was correct, or whether additional terms need to be added.

By classifying each of the referring phrases in the excerpt as shown in Tables 1 and 2, we can obtain the set of domain objects and relations that constitute the framework of the explanation. The *fluid* referred to is isotonic sodium chloride: water with the same concentration of sodium chloride as the blood. Naturally, there will be objects and relations that are represented in the knowledge structure but were not selected for explicit mention in the explanation. We expect that computational constraints will bring these to light as we later construct a model to account for the explanation.

Once its basic terms have been formalized (Table 2), the content of the explanation can be stated explicitly. Table 3 identifies five different statements of causal relationships in the excerpt, falling into two categories. Some of the key objects in the domain (concentrations, forces, and flow rates) are continuously variable quantities, and the subject is asserting facts about those quantities. The first four statements are assertions of structural relationships that hold between certain quantities, without stating anything about the values that they may take on at particular times. The fifth statement refers to the properties that the quantities might take on under particular circumstances, and so describes the behavior of the mechanism.

Our analysis of this excerpt from the transcript, shown in Tables 2 and 3, provides us with the following conclusions, which will serve as empirical constraints on the knowledge representation we devise for the domain knowledge.

TABLE 2. The Complete Set of Objects and Relations Identified in the Excerpt in Table 1.

Substances
  Protein (L162, 170, 174, 179)
  Fluid (L168, 171, 174, 181)

Locations
  Blood vessels (L162, 167, 169, 170, 172, 175, 178, 179)
  Interstitial spaces (L172, 173, 176, 181)

Concentrations
  Concentration (protein, blood) (L162, 179)

Forces
  Hydrostatic pressure (fluid, blood → interstitial spaces) (L164, 167)
  Hydrostatic pressure (fluid, interstitial spaces → blood) (L176–178)
  Serum protein oncotic pressure (fluid, interstitial spaces → blood) (L164, 169–172, 180)
  Interstitial protein oncotic pressure (fluid, blood → interstitial spaces) (L174–175)

Flow rates
  Flow (fluid, blood → interstitial spaces) (L168, 174–175)
  Flow (fluid, interstitial spaces → blood) (L171–172)

TABLE 3. Causal Relationships in the Excerpt[a]

L162   A: When there is a very low albumin in the serum,
L163   there are two forces which cause edema in my thinking—
L164   the hydrostatic and oncotic forces
L165   and we have actually opposed forces,
L166   forces [. . .break. . .] formation is secondary to
L167   the *hydrostatic force* of the blood going through the capillaries
L168   and *causing the transudation of fluid*
L169   as well as the *osmotic force* within the blood vessels
L170   that is *secondary to the proteins* in the plasma
L171   which tend to *draw fluid*
L172   *from the interstitial spaces into the blood vessels*
L173   And also there is the forces *in the extracellular space*
L174   there are *certain proteins* which tend to *pull water*
L175   out of the blood vessels;
L176   and there is a *hydrostatic force* I believe also *in the interstitial spaces*
L177   which can counteract the force of the fluid
L178   coming out from within the vessels. '
L179   And if you have a *very low albumin in the serum*
L180   there will be a *decreased osmotic pressure*
L181   and make it easier for the *fluid to go out into the interstitial spaces*

Descriptions of structure
    Hydrostatic pressure (fluid, blood → interstitial spaces) (L167)
        ⇒ flow (fluid, blood → interstitial spaces) (L168)
    Concentration (protein, blood) (L170)
        ⇒ serum protein oncotic pressure (fluid, interstitial spaces → blood) (L169)
        ⇒ flow (fluid, interstitial spaces → blood) (L171–172)
    Concentration (protein, interstitial spaces) (L174)
        ⇒ flow (fluid, blood → interstitial spaces) (L174–175)
    Hydrostatic pressure (fluid, interstitial spaces → blood) (L176)
        ⇒ flow (fluid, interstitial spaces → blood) (L177–178)

Descriptions of behavior
    Decreased concentration (protein, blood) (L179)
        ⇒ decreased serum protein oncotic pressure (fluid, interstitial spaces → blood) (L180)
        ⇒ increased flow (fluid, blood → interstitial spaces) (L181)

[a]The first four statements describe structural relationships that hold between continuously variable quantities. The fifth describes the behavior of the mechanism.

1. The explanation refers to a relatively small set of objects and relations describing aspects of the domain.
2. Those objects that are involved in the causal assertions are symbolic descriptions of continuously variable quantities or the values they take on at a particular time.
3. Descriptions of the structural relationships making up a mechanism are expressed separately, and therefore probably repre-

sented separately, from descriptions of the dynamic behavior of the mechanism.

4. The symbolic descriptions of quantities and values are stated in qualitative terms: *directions* of flow, *increased* and *decreased* quantities, *low* albumin, *more* perfusion, and so on. This suggests that the symbolic description of quantity and value is stated primarily in terms of ordinal relations among values.

5. THE DOMAIN MODEL—STRUCTURAL DESCRIPTION

At this point, we have extracted the information that is directly available from the transcript. For the next step in our analysis, we must examine the phenomenon itself—in this case the Starling equilibrium—to find a way to represent the structure of its causal relationships. We need a representation for the Starling equilibrium that can support an expert level of inference about its behavior, and that is consistent with the observations we have made. The purpose of the domain model is to make explicit information that is logically necessary to answer questions correctly about the domain, but may not have been stated in the explanation.

We draw on a physiological description of the Starling equilibrium (Valtin, 1973) and express it in a way that is compatible with our observations of the human expert. Our analysis showed that the explanation was stated in terms of *substances* in *locations*, causing *forces* that result in *flows*. We also observed that the objects involved in causal relationships are symbolic descriptions of continuously variable quantities. We begin by defining the possible substances and locations, along with quantities representing their amounts and concentrations, and the constraints among those quantities (Table 4). These constraints among quantities

TABLE 4. Domain Model: Substances, Locations,
Amounts, and Concentrations, and
Some of the Constraints Holding among the Quantities

Substances: protein, fluid
Locations: plasma compartment (P), interstitial compartment (I)
Amounts: $amt(protein,P)$, $amt(protein,I)$, $amt(fluid,P)$, $amt(fluid,I)$
Concentrations: $c(protein,P)$, $c(protein,I)$
Constraints:
　$amt(protein,P) = c(protein,P) * amt(fluid,P)$
　$amt(protein,I) = c(protein,I) * amt(fluid,I)$

---

are what will make it possible to draw new inferences about the state of the equilibrium from a small set of hypotheses.

The Starling equilibrium is an equilibrium involving four forces: the hydrostatic pressures and the oncotic pressures in the two compartments (P and I). There are several different ways to combine the effects of these forces to produce a net flow rate, each with different sets of intermediate terms. We select the combination method that provides the best match with the terms used in stating the causal relations (Table 3). Thus, we combine two pressures of each type to produce net hydrostatic and net oncotic pressures, each of which causes a flow between the two compartments, which are in turn combined to produce a net rate of flow (Table 5).

Other constraints, such as the way the hydrostatic pressure in the blood depends on the amount of fluid in the blood compartment, are very complex and may not be known even to the expert. The physician does, however, know that the functional relationship is strictly monotonically increasing, at least for the situations now being considered. Accordingly, we define a *functional constraint* (M^+) that states that one quantity is an unknown but strictly increasing function of the other. The constraint can be modified (M_0^+) to indicate that the function passes through the origin, as well. In Table 3, we see that the functional con-

TABLE 5. Domain Model: Pressures, Rates of Flow, and
Constraints Holding between Them

Hydrostatic pressures
  HP(fluid,P → I)
  HP(fluid,I → P)
  net HP(fluid,P → I)

Oncotic pressures
  OncP(fluid,I → P)
  OncP(fluid,P → I)
  net OncP(fluid,I → P)

Flow rates
  flow(fluid,P → I)
  flow(fluid,I → P)
  net flow(fluid,P → I)

Constraints (component addition)
  net HP(fluid,P → I) = HP(fluid,P → I) − HP(fluid,I → P)
  net OncP(fluid,I → P) = OncP(fluid,I → P) − OncP(fluid,P → I)
  net flow(fluid,P → I) = flow(fluid,P → I) − flow(fluid,I → P)

TABLE 6. Domain Model: Relationship
between Hydrostatic Pressure and
Amount of Fluid, between Oncotic
Pressure and Protein Concentration, and
between Rate of Flow and Pressure

Constraints (embedded processes)
$HP(fluid, P \rightarrow I) = M^+(amt(fluid, P))$
$HP(fluid, I \rightarrow P) = M^+(amt(fluid, I))$
$OncP(fluid, I \rightarrow P) = M_0^+(c(pr, P))$
$OncP(fluid, P \rightarrow I) = M_0^+(c(pr, I))$
$flow(fluid, P \rightarrow I) = M_0^+(netHP(fluid, P \rightarrow I))$
$flow(fluid, I \rightarrow P) = M_0^+(netOncP(fluid, I \rightarrow P))$

straints correspond to statements giving the direction in which one
quantity depends on another. The fact that a functional relationship is
strictly monotonic provides exactly enough information to support this
inference. Table 6 gives the functional relationships required to model
the Starling equilibrium.

Finally, the rate of flow of fluid from one compartment to another
specifies the rate of change of the amount of fluid in each compartment.
To capture this domain relationship we must formulate and use a *derivative constraint*. There is no specific phrase in the excerpt that we can
identify with the use of a derivative constraint, but such a constraint is
required for computational adequacy of the model.

This system of equations (Tables 4–7) constitutes the domain model
of the structure of the mechanism of the Starling equilibrium. Figure 2 is
a graphical depiction of the structural model, in which the constraint
equations are drawn as linking the quantities involved. Sections 7 and 8
below will discuss the qualitative simulation process whereby this structural model is used to simulate the mechanism's behavior.

Figure 2 makes it relatively easy to see that the four structural asser-

TABLE 7. Domain Model: Rate of Flow
Related to Change in Amount

Constraints (derivative)
$$\frac{d}{dt} amt(fluid, I) = net\ flow(fluid, P \rightarrow I)$$
$$\frac{d}{dt} amt(fluid, P) = -net\ flow(fluid, P \rightarrow I)$$

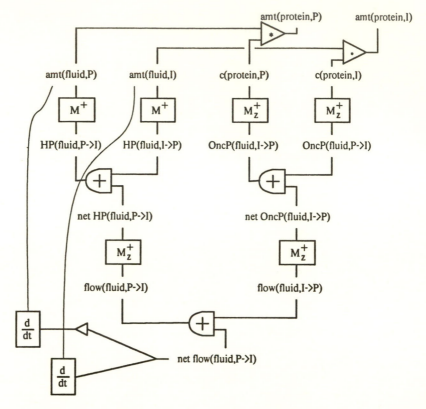

FIGURE 2. The domain model of the Starling equilibrium showing quantities and constraints. At any point in time, the values of the quantities must obey all of the constraints. The system as a whole changes over time while continuing to satisfy the constraints.

tions identified in the explanation correspond to the four branches of the domain model.

6. QUALITATIVE SIMULATION IN THE EXPLANATION

We have constructed a precise model of the structure of the mechanism of the Starling equilibrium. The structural assertions identified in the explanation specify the relevant objects and relations, and some of their connections. Examination of the scientific theory of the domain mechanism allowed us to express those connections precisely as computational constraints without sacrificing the qualitative nature of the explanation.

The next step is to augment the representation until it can carry out a qualitative simulation of the *behavior* of the mechanism, given the qualitative description of its structure. Just as we did with the structural description, we hope to use constraints from the observed explanation, from the computational requirements of the representation, and from knowledge of the domain, to specify the representation and its behavior. When this operation is completed, the portions of the explanation

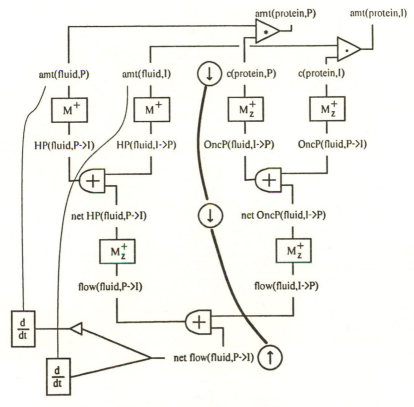

FIGURE 3. The portion of the explanation referring to the behavior of the mechanism can be analyzed as asserting changes to the quantities involved in the structural description (Figure 2).

describing the behavior of the mechanism should correspond with a well-defined part of the qualitative simulation.

We can now make our analysis of the behavioral parts of the explanation more explicit by overlaying the described behavior onto the structural description. Figure 3 shows how the final statement of the explanation can be overlaid onto Figure 2, showing the causal pathway by which loss of plasma protein causes a shift in the Starling equilibrium, thus translocating fluid from the plasma into the interstitial space.

The effect of the change to the Starling equilibrium is primarily to reduce the plasma volume, which in turn causes the kidney to retain salt and water rather than excreting them. The Starling equilibrium continues to shift much of this additional fluid into the tissues, causing the visible swelling of the appendages. In the excerpt below, the subject is explaining this latter process, using only behavioral statements. Table 8 shows the excerpt and its analysis, and Figure 4 shows the qualitative changes overlaid onto the same domain model. This analysis of the transcript helps specify the behavior we want from the simulation process, and gives us confidence that the terms chosen for the structural description are correct.

TABLE 8. Physician Explaining the Hypothetical Consequences
of *Increased* Salt Intake, Which Would Result in Increased Fluid Retention,
and Hence Increased Edema[a]

L215   The hydrostatic pressure now will increase.
L216   The tissues will be perfused more,
L217   and because of the increased osm . . . hydrostatic pressure within the vessels,
L218   and the decreased osmotic pressure,
L219   that is the decreased albumin also within the vessels,
L220   we'll get a transudation of fluid, that is, salt water,
L221   from the vessels into the interstitium.

Description of behavior
  increased hydrostatic pressure(fluid, blood → interstitial spaces) (L215)
    ⇒ increased flow(fluid, blood → interstitial spaces) (L216)
  increased hydrostatic pressure(fluid, blood → intersitital spaces) (L217)
    ⇒ increased flow(fluid, blood → interstitial spaces) (L220–221)
  decreased amount(protein, blood) (L219)
    ⇒ decreased oncotic pressure(fluid, interstitial spaces → blood) (L218)
    ⇒ increased flow(fluid, blood → interstitial spaces) (L220–221)

---

[a]The fragment shown here is only the portion of the explanation that deals with the Starling equilibrium.

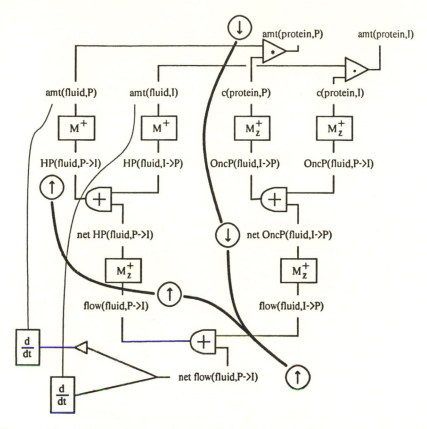

FIGURE 4. The trace of the behavior described in Table 8 is overlaid onto the domain model.

7. THE DOMAIN MODEL—QUALITATIVE DESCRIPTION OF STATE

The fifth statement in the explanation describes the behavior of the mechanism. By examining the relations described in the transcript, and attempting to maintain logical adequacy, we can propose a representation for the dynamic state of the qualitative simulation, and for the inference rules that drive it.

One conspicuous characteristic of the transcript is the qualitative vocabulary used to describe quantities: *directions* of flow, *increased* and *decreased* quantities, *low* albumin, *more* perfusion, and so on. This suggests that the simulation works primarily with *ordinal relations* among the values of the quantities in the structural domain model: E.g., a quantity is *increased* if its current value is greater than its previous (or its normal) value. The numerical values of particular quantities (e.g., plasma oncotic pressure) at different times are unspecified and sometimes unknown to the physician. Thus, the knowledge representation must function with *descriptions* of values, not with the numerical values themselves. Since all that is mentioned about those values are their ordinal relationships, we might conclude that the description of a value consists of exactly its ordinal relationships with other values.

Logical adequacy, however, requires us to distinguish between two closely related concepts: (1) the *ordinal relation* between two values—greater-than, equal, less-than; (2) the *direction of change* of a single value over time—increasing, steady, decreasing. A patient's current blood pressure, for example, could be in any one of the nine states combining these two attributes, with different clinical significance in each case. Therefore, the qualitative description of a value must contain both its ordinal relations with other values and its direction of change. The logical necessity of this distinction forces us to include it in any representation for expert causal reasoning, even though the two concepts are difficult to distinguish in the transcript.

This qualitative description in terms of ordinal relations provides a powerful representation for partial knowledge of a collection of related quantities. The representation is rich in states of partial knowledge: Where little is known, it is possible to express precisely what is known without having to make additional assumptions or discard useful information (Kuipers, 1979). On the other hand, if there are many "landmark" values of a quantity, then ordinal relationships can specify where the current value lies with respect to the landmarks and provide arbitrarily high resolution.

The constraint types defined above for the structural description interact almost perfectly with these qualitative descriptions of value. Essentially, each constraint acts as a local theorem-prover operating in an unquantified relational calculus, having access to its own axioms and the information known about the associated quantities, and communicating with its neighbors through shared quantities. For example, the constraint $X + Y = Z$ makes inferences of the form:

If $X_1 > 0$ and $Y_1 = 0$ then $Z_1 > 0$.
If $X_1 > X_2$ and $Z_1 = Z_2$ then $Y_1 < Y_2$.
If *decreasing*(X_1) and *steady*(Z_1) then *increasing*(Y_1).

Kuipers (1984) defines this representation in detail, based on a design by Steele (1980) that operates on integer values.

This propagation of information through constraints does not correspond to a sequence of events taking place over time. Rather, we start with a small amount of information about the current state of the mechanism and deduce a much more complete description of the state of the mechanism at the same point in time. The actual simulation process analyzes the configuration of changing values to predict the next state after the passage of time (Kuipers, 1984). These two processes correspond to two different senses of "causality." In the first, one assertion is logically subsequent to the other, but temporally simultaneous. In the second case, the second assertion both logically and temporally follows the first.

8. THE DOMAIN MODEL—QUALITATIVE SIMULATION

The propagation of information across the constraints provides an increasingly complete description of the state of the mechanism at a particular point in time, deriving new information about its intermediate variables. Once a sufficiently well-specified description of the current state exists, the simulation process examines the configuration of changing values to determine what can be asserted about the next state whose qualitative description is distinct from the current one. The propagation process then begins again for this new time-point, until yet another state can be determined. De Kleer (1977) introduced the term *envisionment* for this process. The qualitative simulation system has been implemented and is described in detail in Kuipers (1984).

The rules for determining the next qualitatively distinct state are elaborations on the following two types of qualitative changes, which depend on the ordinal relationship between the current value of a quantity and nearby "landmarks" or distinguished values.

- *Move from Distinguished Value:* If the current value of a changing quantity is equal to a distinguished value, then let the next value be an undistinguished value perturbed in the direction of change, closer to the starting point than any other distinguished value.
- *Move to Limit:* If the current value of a changing quantity is not equal to a distinguished value, and there is a distinguished value in the direction of change, let the value of that quantity in the next time-point be equal to the next distinguished value.

The subject's goal in his explanation is to show how the Starling equilibrium contributes to edema in the nephrotic syndrome (Table 1, L162–163). Our hypothesis is that the explanation is derived from the qualitative simulation of the Starling equilibrium mechanism, based on its structural description. The result we want the explanation to justify is:

$$amt(protein,P) < normal \Rightarrow amt(fluid,I) > normal$$

Table 9 shows the result of envisioning the Starling equilibrium. We assume that the reasoning system has, from its previous knowledge of nephrology, a description of the normal state of the Starling mechanism in equilibrium. State (N) in Table 9 represents that normal state; the term *norm* in each line refers to the normal value of *that* quantity, to simplify the notation. State (1) is created by asserting the initial conditions defining the nephrotic syndrome:

> $amt(protein,P) < normal$ and held constant,
> $amt(protein,I) = normal$ and held constant,
> $amt(fluid,P) = normal$,
> $amt(fluid,I) = normal$.

TABLE 9. Use of the Envisionment to Show That
$amt(protein,P) < normal \Rightarrow amt(fluid,I) > normal$[a]

Quantity	(N)	(1)	(2)	(3)
amt(protein,P)	= norm(std)	< norm(const)	< norm(const)	< norm(const)
amt(protein,I)	= norm(std)	= norm(const)	= norm(const)	= norm(const)
amt(fluid,P)	= norm(std)	= norm(dec)	< norm(dec)	< norm(std)
amt(fluid,I)	= norm(std)	= norm(inc)	> norm(inc)	> norm(std)
c(protein,P)	= norm(std)	< norm(inc)	< norm(inc)	< norm(std)
c(protein,I)	= norm(std)	= norm(dec)	< norm(dec)	< norm(std)
HP(fluid,I → P)	= norm(std)	= norm(inc)	> norm(inc)	> norm(std)
HP(fluid,P → I)	= norm(std)	= norm(dec)	< norm(dec)	< norm(std)
netHP(fluid,P → I)	= norm(std)	= norm(dec)	< norm(dec)	< norm(std)
OncP(fluid,I → P)	= norm(std)	< norm(inc)	< norm(inc)	< norm(std)
OncP(fluid,P → I)	= norm(std)	= norm(dec)	< norm(dec)	< norm(std)
netOncP(fluid,I → P)	= norm(std)	< norm(inc)	< norm(inc)	< norm(std)
flow(fluid,I → P)	= norm(std)	< norm(inc)	< norm(inc)	= f* < norm(std)
flow(fluid,P → I)	= norm(std)	= norm(dec)	< norm(dec)	= f* < norm(std)
net flow(fluid,P → I)	= 0(std)	> 0(dec)	> 0(dec)	= 0(std)

[a] *norm* refers to the normal value of *that* quantity; initial inequalities propagate to provide ordinal relations; derivative constraints provide directions of change, which then propagate; state (1) ⇒ (2) as many values move from distinguished values; state (2) ⇒ (3) as the collision, *flow(fluid,I → P) = flow(fluid,P → I)* precedes any other qualitative change.

Thereafter, the propagation process completes the description of state (1). The simulation process asserts new ordinal relations in state (2) for each changing quantity in state (1), and propagation adds the directions of change to complete the description of state (2). The simulation process must diagnose which of several qualitative changes take place after state (2). It concludes that the first qualitative change is the one that makes *net flow(fluid,P → I)* = 0, but leaves all other changing quantities different from their previous normal values. The propagation process fills in the directions of change (all *steady*) to show that state (3) is an equilibrium.

Examining the qualitative values in Table 9, we see that the original goal was achieved, of explaining the link:

$$amt(protein,P) < normal \Rightarrow amt(fluid,I) > normal$$

since the antecedent of this causal link was asserted as an initial condition, and the consequent holds true in the final equilibrium state. An additional important feature of this simulation process is the fact that many other facts are derived and stored about the states of the other variables in the mechanism. These other variables are critical as the interfaces to other physiological mechanisms. In this case, the value of *amt(fluid,P)* in state (3) acts as the interface with the total body fluid equilibrium.

The requirement of computational adequacy tells us that the reasoning process must carry out this simulation in order for the reasoner to predict the behavior of the mechanism. It must produce a wealth of detail in order to interface correctly with the many other mechanisms in human physiology. On the other hand, a careful examination of the behavioral assertion in Table 3 and its overlay representation in Figure 3 shows that the content of the subject's explanation is derived solely from the propagation of information through the network to complete state (1). A possible explanation for this is that the qualitative simulation is both complicated to express and capable of running to conclusion on its own, so the most effective explanation omits the simulation trace.

9. CONCLUSION

We have followed the derivation of a working computer simulation of an aspect of causal reasoning from end to end. The first part of the chapter demonstrates a methodology for collecting and analyzing observations of experts at work, in order to find the conceptual framework used for the particular domain. The second part of the chapter developed a representation for qualitative knowledge of the structure and behavior of a mechanism. The qualitative simulation, or envisionment, process is given a qualitative structural description of a mechanism along with initialization information, and produces a detailed description of the mechanism's behavior.

By following the construction of a knowledge representation from the identification of the problem to the running computer simulation, this discussion provides a "vertical" slice of the construction of a cognitive model. It demonstrates an effective knowledge acquisition method for the purpose of determining the structure of the representation itself, not simply the content of the knowledge to be encoded in that representation. Most important, it demonstrates the interaction among constraints derived from textbook knowledge of the domain, from observations of the human expert, and from the computational requirements of successful performance.

The knowledge representation for causal reasoning is presented in greater detail in Kuipers (1984), along with several examples in nonmedical domains that reveal more of its interesting properties. Since the objects of the representation are descriptions of continuously variable quantities, and their relationships are expressed as arithmetic, derivative, or functional relations, the resulting models look very similar to physiological models in the style of Guyton *et al.* (1973) or systems dynamics models in the style of Forrester (1969). One might ask how the models differ, and whether we could avoid the analysis of transcripts and create the models directly from the scientific literature in physiology.

The detailed analysis of physician behavior suggested the *level of description* for the causal models: the set of qualitative relationships and their inference rules that can express incomplete knowledge while remaining able to draw useful conclusions about behavior. Once we have determined an appropriate qualitative representation, it is possible that existing techniques for acquiring knowledge in expert systems (Davis, 1982) will be adequate to specify the content of the models using input from human experts and from the scientific literature.

The representation presented here differs from the Guyton and Forrester models in its ability to express a larger, more flexible set of states of partial knowledge. In particular, the functional constraints M^+ and M^- express functional relationships known to be monotonic in a specific direction but otherwise unknown. Furthermore, the simulation based on this structural description is not limited to precisely specified numerical values but can operate on symbolic descriptions that constrain the possible numerical values a quantity could take on at a particular time.

Another important difference is how the use of the model influences its size and its scope. When the laboratory scientist formulates a Guyton-style model to account for a phenomenon, he attempts to include every possible factor and relationship that influences the mechanism, so the models tend to become very large. An expert physician reasoning about a case uses only those factors he considers particularly relevant, and thus is able to restrict his attention to a much smaller model. To make up for the lack of detail, the expert must then have many different small models, each with its own assumptions and thus expressing different "points of view." The causal model representation is intended to express this highly modularized knowledge structure, so its models will typically be relatively small. Indeed, it appears that there is a fortunate match between the limited working memory and processing capacity of the human and the inability of the causal model representation to handle very large models.

This representation for the structure and behavior of a mechanism is intended to express descriptions that are strictly weaker than the corresponding differential equation, in the sense that several different differential equations would be consistent with a single causal model. Figure 5 shows the ideal relationship between the two descriptive systems.

Having found the causal model representation by detailed study of

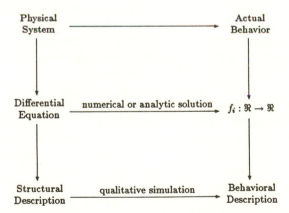

FIGURE 5. The qualitative structural description is capable of capturing more partial states of knowledge than differential equations, and produces a partial description of the mechanism's behavior. Because the qualitative simulation occasionally uses heuristics, the two paths through the diagram do not necessarily yield the same result.

the behavior of human experts, we can return to the suggestion that we concentrate on the medical facts of the domain as captured in the medical literature. The fact that the causal model is strictly weaker than the corresponding differential equation model may allow us to construct and validate truly large medical knowledge bases. It suggests the possibility that causal models might be constructed by systematically transforming precise models from the scientific literature into the weaker causal model representation. The resulting causal models would then constitute the knowledge base. Weakening the descriptive language allows the system to reason effectively with the type of mixed qualitative and quantitative information that is typically available to physicians. Much more work is needed before this method can be tested and realized, but it is an attractive alternative to the current slow and unverifiable methods for constructing large knowledge bases.

10. POSTSCRIPT

10.1. COMPUTER IMPLEMENTATION

As frequently happens in mathematics and computer science, the qualitative simulation algorithm that was inspired by these studies of human experts, and described here and in Kuipers (1984), has led to the development of a new, improved model. The QSIM algorithm (Kuipers, 1985) uses the same qualitative representation for structural constraints and derives the same type of behavioral description, but its processing strategy makes it unlikely to be an accurate cognitive model of human expert reasoning about the behavior of mechanisms. On the other hand, it has the clear mathematical relation with ordinary differential equations that we had hoped for in Figure 5. It is also very efficient, making it a useful knowledge engineering tool. Kuipers and Kassirer (1985) demonstrate some of the applications of qualitative simulation to reasoning about mechanisms in medical physiology.

10.2. TYPES OF ANALYSIS

Thus far, in this work and other research to be reported elsewhere, we have found several different useful kinds of protocol analysis. These are types of analysis to apply to the same raw data—the verbatim transcript—to answer different questions about the underlying knowledge representation.

- *Referring phrase analysis* identifies the set of referring phrases in a protocol excerpt and defines a small natural universe of underlying conceptual objects that can be the referents of those phrases. This is particularly important for determining the primitive elements of the knowledge representation.
- *Assertional analysis* identifies the set of assertions being made in the excerpt about the objects identified by referring phrase analysis. A set of relations on objects and connectives and operators on sentences are then defined to express the content of the assertions.
- *Script analysis* identifies the overall structure of the reasoning process, argument, or explanation being given in the excerpt. The analysis is intended to reveal the goal structure of the problem-solving process or the explanation strategy. This helps to determine the control structure of the inference process that operates on the knowledge representation.

There are certainly other types of analysis as well. Ericsson and Simon (1984) provide an authoritative treatment of protocol analysis.

10.3. GUIDELINES SUMMARY

As this chapter demonstrates, analysis of verbatim transcripts is both time-intensive and expertise-intensive, but it yields a detailed picture of the representation of the expert's knowledge that is difficult to obtain any other way. The analysis involves a painstaking examination of the transcript, applying expert knowledge of both the problem domain and the space of known computational methods for solving problems. Protocol analysis is a highly active and intellectually demanding process because it involves continually generating and matching computational models of the inferences seen in each fragment of the transcript. Thus, the main portions of the analysis cannot be performed automatically or by clerical assistants.

Protocol analysis is inherently an analysis of the individual subject and is thus vulnerable to biases derived from the idiosyncracies of the individual. The methodology does not lend itself to aggregation of raw data across a population of subjects. However, this is appropriate in gathering evidence toward the design of an AI program, for two reasons. First, an AI program inherently behaves as an individual. It has its own state of knowledge reflecting its own history of acquired knowledge and inferences performed. Thus, if we create an AI program as a cognitive model, it models some abstract individual, not the average properties of a class. Second, the fine structure of a knowledge representation is obscured when data are aggregated across subjects, owing precisely to the individual variation among humans. If we wish to have a clear view of the structure of knowledge, our only hope is to look at individuals and only later learn to recognize and account for individual variation.

The methods described here are exploratory techniques, appropriate for guiding the discovery of new knowledge representation hypotheses. Since there are many domains of knowledge where we know little about the underlying representation, these methods can be useful. Thus, the cognitive scientist uses protocol analysis as one way to *discover* knowledge representation hypotheses that might be *testable* using more traditional methods. The knowledge engineer might use protocol analysis to motivate the selection or design of a knowledge representation for an expert system and its knowledge base. Once a particular knowledge representation is selected, other methods may be more appropriate and cost-effective for building up a large knowledge base. As artificial intelligence makes the transition from an art to a science, these protocol analysis methods may contribute to the developments of real disciplines of knowledge engineering and cognitive science.

ACKNOWLEDGMENTS. This research was supported in part by grants to the first author from the National Library of Medicine (NIH R01 LM 04125, LM 04374, and LM 04515), and from the National Science Foundation (MCS-8303640, DCR-8417934, and DCR-8512779).

11. REFERENCES

Chi, M. T. H., Feltovich, P. J., and Glaser, R. (1982). Categorization and representation of physics problems by experts and novices. *Cognitive Science, 5*, 121–152.

Davis, R. (1982). Teiresias: Applications of meta-level knowledge. In R. Davis and D. B. Lenat, *Knowledge-based systems in artificial intelligence*. New York: McGraw-Hill.

de Dombal, F. T., Leaper, D. J., Staniland, J. R., McCann, A. P., and Horrocks, J. C. (1972). Computer-aided diagnosis of abdominal pain. *British Medical Journal, 2*, 9–13.

de Kleer, J. (1977). Multiple representations of knowledge in a mechanics problem-solver. *Proceedings of the Fifth International Joint Conference on Artificial Intelligence.*

de Kleer, J. (1979). The origin and resolution of ambiguities in causal arguments. *Proceedings of the Sixth International Joint Conference on Artificial Intelligence.*

de Kleer, J., and Brown, J. S. (1984). A qualitative physics based on confluences. *Artificial Intelligence, 24*, 7–83.

Elstein, A. S., Shulman, L. S., and Sprafka, S. A. (1978). *Medical problem solving: An analysis of clinical reasoning*. Cambridge, Mass.: Harvard University Press.

Ericsson, K. A., and Simon, H. A. (1980). Verbal reports as data. *Psychological Review, 87,* 215–251.

Ericsson, K. A., and Simon, H. A. (1984). *Protocol analysis.* Cambridge, Mass.: M.I.T. Press.

Forbus, K. D. (1981). Qualitative reasoning about physical processes. *Proceedings of the Seventh International Joint Conference on Artificial Intelligence.*

Forbus, K. D. (1984). Qualitative process theory. *Artificial Intelligence, 24,* 85–168.

Forrester, J. (1969). *Urban dynamics.* Cambridge, Mass.: M.I.T. Press.

Guyton, A. C., Jones, C. E., and Coleman, T. G. (1973). *Circulatory physiology: Cardiac output and its regulation* (2nd ed.). Philadelphia: W. B. Saunders.

Kassirer, J. P., and Gorry, G. A. (1978). Clinical problem solving: A behavioral analysis. *Annals of Internal Medicine, 89,* 245–255.

Kassirer, J. P., Kuipers, B. J., and Gorry, G. A. (1982). Toward a theory of clinical expertise. *American Journal of Medicine, 73,* 251–259.

Kuipers, B. J. (1979). On representing commonsense knowledge. In N. V. Findler (Ed.), *Associative networks: The representation and use of knowledge by computers.* New York: Academic Press.

Kuipers, B. J. (1982). Getting the envisionment right. *Proceedings of the National Conference on Artificial Intelligence (AAAI-82).*

Kuipers, B. J. (1984). Commonsense reasoning about causality: Deriving behavior from structure. *Artificial Intelligence, 24,* 169–204.

Kuipers, B. J. (1985). The limits of qualitative simulation. *Proceedings of the Ninth International Joint Conference on Artificial Intelligence (IJCAI-85).*

Kuipers, B. J., and Kassirer, J. P. (1985). Qualitative simulation in medical physiology: A progress report. Cambridge, Mass.: MIT Laboratory for Computer Science TM-280.

Larkin, J., McDermott, J., Simon, D. P., and Simon, H. A. (1980). Expert and novice performance in solving physics problems. *Science, 208,* 1335–1342.

Newell, A., and Simon, H. A. (1972). *Human problem solving.* Englewood Cliffs, N.J.: Prentice-Hall.

Nisbett, R. E., and Wilson, T. D. (1977). Telling more than we can know: Verbal reports on mental processes. *Psychological Review, 84,* 231–259.

Patil, R. S. (1981). *Causal representation of patient illness for electrolyte and acid-base diagnosis.* Cambridge, Mass.: MIT Laboratory for Computer Science TR-267.

Pople, H. E., Jr. (1982). Heuristic methods for imposing structure on ill structured problems: The structuring of medical diagnostics. In P. Szolovits (Ed.), *Artificial intelligence in medicine.* Boulder, Co.: AAAS/Westview Press.

Rimoldi, H. J. A. (1961). The test of diagnostic skills. *Journal of Medical Education, 36,* 73.

Steele, G. L., Jr. (1980). *The definition and implementation of a computer programming language based on constraints.* Cambridge, Mass.: MIT Artificial Intelligence Laboratory TR-595.

Valtin, H. (1973). *Renal function: Mechanisms preserving fluid and solute balance in health.* Boston: Little, Brown.

4

A Systematic Study of Knowledge Base Refinement in the Diagnosis of Leukemia

JOHN FOX, CHRISTOPHER D. MYERS,
MELVYN F. GREAVES, and SUSAN PEGRAM

1. INTRODUCTION

Expert systems were first recognizable in their contemporary form in medicine, and medicine is still among the largest nonmilitary areas of expert system application. In this field, however, few have entered routine service. Many observers of expert systems say that the acquisition of knowledge is the major obstacle to success in building these systems (e.g., Hayes-Roth *et al.*, 1983). In medicine, on the other hand, there is evidence that knowledge acquisition can be rapid (e.g., Mulsant and Servan-Schreiber, 1984) and the reasons for the systems' slow introduction are more complex, ranging from their intrinsic clinical versatility to political factors (e.g., Fox, 1984a).

It is alarming that although there are useful commentaries on

JOHN FOX • Biomedical Computing Unit, Imperial Cancer Research Fund, London WC2A 3PX, England.   CHRISTOPHER D. MYERS • Biomedical Computing Unit, Imperial Cancer Research Fund, London WC2A 3PX, England, and Department of Microbiology, University of Texas, Dallas, Texas 75235.   MELVYN F. GREAVES and SUSAN PEGRAM • The Leukaemia Research Fund Centre, Institute for Cancer Research, London SW3 6JB, England.

knowledge acquisition methods (e.g., Welbank, 1983), there are few objective results to guide designers in the selection of knowledge acquisition techniques, anticipation of problems, or estimation of progress. Since in the present state of the art we can neither use entirely formal methods for the construction of knowledge bases nor guarantee consistency, completeness, or correctness of knowledge bases, we need to try to ensure quality in some other way. This chapter identifies some points where problems can creep in during a "commonsense" knowledge acquisition procedure, but suggests ways in which they may be reduced.

Medicine continues to offer an important developing ground for expert system techniques. This is partly because of the complex challenges offered by the subject, but also because of the traditional demand within medicine for objective, quantitative demonstrations of the value of techniques. The domain of application for the present study was leukemia diagnosis, but we believe that the results have general significance for knowledge-based classification systems, and that quantitative analysis of system performance trends should always be considered.

2. LEUKEMIA DIAGNOSIS

Developments in immunology and hematology have provided ways of classifying leukemias that help to predict the course of the disease and guide treatment decisions. Leukemias are classified according to the clinical aggressiveness of the disease (acute or chronic), by the hematological class of the leukemia (lymphoid or myeloid), and by cell surface immunology data obtained by laboratory tests (Figure 1). In essence, leukemic cells can be classified by their sensitivity to monoclonal antibodies and other reagents. Fluorescent markers are used to signal the uptake of antibody by the cells and thereby indicate the presence of certain cell surface proteins in cell populations.

In the ICRF Membrane Immunology Laboratory (now the Leukaemia Research Fund Centre) batteries of monoclonal antibodies and other tests have been used routinely to analyze tissue samples, sometimes involving two dozen tests on a sample. Each test result represents the percentage of cells that are positive to the reagent. The pattern of antibody uptake can indicate the presence or absence of disease, and the particular type of leukemia when disease is present. Diagnosis is made from these test results together with items of hematological information and clinical information when available.

The outcome of the testing and interpretation is a brief report, indi-

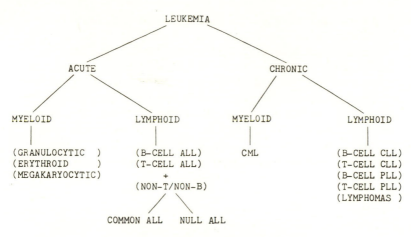

FIGURE 1. The different types of leukemia.

cating the expected type of leukemia, often with various qualifying remarks (e.g., "definitely," "compatible with") or a statement to the effect
that the case is "undiagnosable." The interpretation of the data patterns, however, requires expertise that is possessed by only a handful of
individuals.

The ICRF laboratory was an international center for research into
leukemia and the analysis of this type of data. Our expert advisor (the
third author, now Director of the Leukaemia Research Fund Centre,
London) was head of the laboratory and an acknowledged authority in
the leukemia field. He was the final authority on the interpretation of
test data from the clinical samples received by the laboratory. At present
there is no independent basis for making diagnoses that is more definitive than this expert's judgment.

3. KNOWLEDGE ELICITATION AND EXPERT SYSTEM
   DEVELOPMENT

One purpose of our project was to attempt to answer the question
of whether an expert system could assist in test interpretation. If the
answer is yes, then diagnosis of the disease could be routinely carried
out in hospitals and health centers equipped with the necessary biological reagents and with an expert system to analyze the test results.
However, we were also conscious of the need for a systematic approach
to system development and quality control, and therefore we also decid-

ed to take the opportunity of studying, and analyzing the value of, our knowledge acquisition technique.

We considered several approaches to knowledge acquisition at the beginning of this project. The choice was broadly between informal "hand crafting" of the knowledge base and some automatic or semi-automatic techniques for compiling the knowledge base. We felt that the automated techniques were immature and suffered from implicit assumptions built into the algorithm or statistical methods used (e.g., Fox, 1985). For this study, therefore, we decided on an informal method: the elicitation of knowledge from an expert colleague by analyzing spoken commentaries obtained while he worked.

Tape recordings were made of M.G. diagnosing cases of leukemia from written laboratory records. (A spoken commentary is frequently given for explanations and teaching other staff.) Diagnoses are always made from written clinical and laboratory data alone; the patients are never seen. Laboratory records for 63 patients were selected on the grounds that the tests had been carried out as part of an international trial with an agreed protocol, and that the testing had been carried out at more than one center. The records, which will be referred to as the transcript set, included data of varying completeness and quality. The 63 diagnoses took about 5 hours over two sessions. The recordings included occasional clarifying questions from the first two authors, who sat in on the sessions, and M.G.'s answers to them. Verbatim transcripts were made of the tapes.

Material for the leukemia system's knowledge base was extracted from the transcripts in stages. First, statements in the transcripts that appeared to contain substantive information were highlighted and were extracted from the files with a text editor. Second, the statements were simplified to represent the basic relationships being described, and duplications were removed. A typical transcript and its highlighted and simplified forms are illustrated in Figure 2. Finally, the simplified list was refined into a table of *If . . . then* rules for addition to the expert system package.

3.1. EXPERT SYSTEM PACKAGE

The EMYCIN expert system package was used for the study. EMYCIN is derived from, and has many features in common with, the well-known MYCIN system, the first medical expert system (Shortliffe, 1976). MYCIN introduced many of the features that are now common in expert systems, including the representation of knowledge as *If . . . then* production rules, probabilistic parameters attached to the rules, application

MG: This patient is a 50 year old adult who in common with the last patient
was said to have chronic myeloid leukemia diagnosed in 1978 and has now gone
into blastic transformation and is said to be lymphoid by morphological and
cytochemical criteria. ... Looking at bone marrow which has 70 % BLASTS. Um
I also know, though I can't give a numerical value to it, that when this
value of 70 % is obtained from a smear of blood then in the process of doing
the marker tests there is an ENRICHMENT OF BLASTS, SO 70 % MAY BE A MINIMUM
value and there may be rather more. TERMINAL TRANSFERASE IS 90 %. IN FACT THERE
HAS BEEN SOME ENRICHMENT, SINCE IN AN ADULT THIS IS A LEUKEMIA MARKER. An ADULT
PATIENT WITH NORMAL TdT POSITIVE CELLS ARE NOT MORE THAN 5 %. So this is ...
are all leukemic lymphoblasts in lymphoblastic transformation of CML rather
than myeloblastic. And I'm looking to see what subset it is - 90 % the
IMMUNOGLOBULIN IS ONLY 4 % SO ITS NOT B. T-CELL MARKERS ARE 14 %, 5 %, 6 % AND
LESS THAN 1 %. ALL LESS THAN 20. YOU COULD SAY THAT 90 % OVERLAPS WITH 14 % BUT
I REGARD THAT AS AN INSIGNIFICANT OVERLAP ... WITHIN THE ERROR OF OUR
TECHNIQUES.

a

. 70 % blasts, preparation gives enrichment of blasts, so 70 % may be a
  minimum
. Terminal transferase is 90 %. In fact there has been some enrichment,
. since in an adult this is a leukemia marker. An adult patient with
  normal TdT positive cells are not more than 5 %
. immunoglobulin is only 4 % so its not B.
. T-cell markers are 14 %, 5 %, 6 % and less than 1 %. All less than 20. You
  could say that 90 % overlaps with 14 % but I regard that as an
  insignificant overlap ... within the error of our techniques.

b

. preparation enriches for blasts, so take blast count to be minimum
. Tdt blast count --> suggests enrichment
. Tdt in adult --> leukemic marker
. normal adult level of tdt less than 5 %
. immunoglobulin <5 % --> not B-cells
. T-cell markers less than 20 % --> not T-cells
. overlap of 14 with 90 --> insignificant

c

FIGURE 2. (a) Abstract from original transcript; "substantive" information is shown in
block capitals. (b) Extracted statements from original transcript. (c) Statements from final
distillation of transcripts.

of the rules during reasoning by means of backward chaining, rudimentary capabilities of the system to explain its behavior and conclusions,
and so forth.

EMYCIN incorporates extensive facilities for knowledge base development and refinement, as well as the rule interpreter and other run-
time facilities (van Melle, 1980). The package seemed a good choice for
our study because it has been influential and is widely known; it has
been used successfully by a number of groups for a variety of expert
system applications.

3.2. System Development

The first step in system development was to get a rough view of the leukemia diagnosis task. Some general orientation prior to system building is as necessary in knowledge engineering as it is in software engineering. Furthermore, it is mandatory in developing an EMYCIN system. An EMYCIN consultation has a form that is determined by a hierarchical structure called the context tree. The context tree is used for organizing data that have been entered by the user or inferred by the system. A leukemia context tree could include any number of concepts. These might include concepts like "patient," "samples" for the patient, "clinical findings," laboratory "tests" on the samples, "sets" of tests (where tests are repeated, for example), and so on. The context tree has a substantial influence on the behavior of an EMYCIN system, and it must be designed and installed before a knowledge base can be developed.

It turned out that there were few clues to be found in the transcripts as to the appropriate structure for the context tree, or how to employ it. After discussion with M.G., and some trials and errors, a structure consisting of two major entities, person and sample, was adopted. This context tree, together with its associated parameters, is presented in Figure 3. "Sample" refers to the sample of blood, bone marrow, or cerebrospinal fluid that is sent to the laboratory (occasionally there is more than one). For each sample we treated the diagnosis decision as involving two subdecisions, establishing the cell lineage and the cell type. Blood cells differentiate into different lines (e.g., myeloid and lymphoid) and go through various stages or types in their development. The diagnosis reflects both the line and type of the cells that are proliferating.

3.3. Knowledge Base Development

Once the context tree had been installed, we set about developing the knowledge base using the knowledge table derived from the transcripts. This was done in phases, in order to keep any different stages of knowledge addition that might emerge distinct, and in order to provide test points over which performance trends could be monitored. Six significantly different knowledge bases have been developed. As each stage was completed, a copy of the system was set aside ("frozen") for future study. The development of these six systems is summarized below.

1. A system of 21 rules was assembled quickly from the knowledge table before any organizational issues were encountered.

```
ROOT CONTEXT:         PERSON

    Parameters:                 PERSON-NAME             (Initialdata)
                                SEX                     (Initialdata)
                                AGE                     (Initialdata)
                                PROVISIONAL DIAGNOSIS
                                MEDIASTINAL MASS
                                PHILADELPHIA-CHROMOSOME
                                AGE GROUP

                                DIAGNOSIS               (Goal Parameter)


DESCENDENT CONTEXT:   SAMPLE

    Parameters:                 SAMPLE TYPE             (Initialdata)
                                BLAST COUNT             (Initialdata)

                                AUER BODIES
                                BLOOD COUNT
                                C-ALL
                                E-ROS
                                HLA-DR
                                KAPPA
                                LAMBDA
                                MOUSE-ROSETTES
                                SMIG
                                TDT
                                WT1

                                B-CELLS
                                E ROS NEG T CELL
                                EXPANDED-POP
                                T-CELLS

                                CELL LINEAGE            (Goal Parameter)
                                CELL TYPE               (Goal Parameter)
```

FIGURE 3. The structure of the leukemia system context tree. Contexts are the main entities of the domain. The objective of a consultation is to derive values for the Goal parameter of the Root Context, using the relevant rules. This in turn will require the tracing of values of other parameters of PERSON, and all SAMPLES. In the Leukaemia System the values for the DIAGNOSIS parameter depend on the values of CELL LINEAGE and CELL TYPE, and a DIAGNOSIS of UNDIAGNOSABLE is concluded if all the appropriate rules fail. (An Initial Data parameter is one whose value is always asked of the user whenever a new instance of that context is created.)

2. Thirteen rules were added, 12 directly from the knowledge table and the 13th after discussion of a particular point with M.G. Three rules were also modified.

3. Fifteen rules were added, and two were modified.

4. At this point a prospective series of 100 patients was introduced as a test set, and the performance of the 49-rule system was assessed on both the transcript set and the new test set. As a result, 10 rules were added, 1 discarded, and 1 modified.

5. At this stage, approximately 35% of the original knowledge table was still unused, though the main factors were thought to have been covered. The fifth version was largely developed from this unused, more detailed information. Nine new rules were added and one modified.
6. The final system was primarily developed in response to testing on the new series of 100 patients. One new parameter and 15 new rules had been added, 4 old rules deleted, and 5 others modified.

The transcripts are mainly qualitative. Some quantitative facts were mentioned, such as test result thresholds, and a few rough expressions of probability (e.g., "few of these patients are elderly"; "about a third of acute lymphoid leukemias are negative to this test"). Probabilities must be handled with particular care. EMYCIN incorporates a mechanism for imprecise reasoning by revising numerical measures of belief and disbelief in hypotheses, as rules are applied to data. The designer may attach a "certainty factor" to any rule, representing the strength of the inference that the rule makes. Certainty factors were supplied by C.D.M. in consultation with M.G.

4. SYSTEM PERFORMANCE

The performance of the various systems was assessed by comparing the diagnoses with M.G.'s recorded judgements for each case. In leukemia, as in many if not all medical pathologies, it is usually impossible to achieve an objective diagnosis due to the lack of unambiguous features. The only "gold standard" of performance is the conclusion made by the expert. This may not seem wholly satisfactory, but since our eventual goal is to transfer M.G.'s expertise to a computerized system available to less specialized medical personnel, the system's ability to emulate his decisions is the only practical measure of its performance (Buchanan and Shortliffe, 1984, Chapter 30).

Since the diagnosis may consist of several parts (cell lineage, cell type, etc.), several criteria were used to assess each diagnostic decision:

CORRECT   Answer agrees exactly with M.G.'s answer.

INCORRECT   A decision is made that contradicts M.G.'s diagnosis.

CORRECT + OTHER   A list of options including "correct" and "incorrect" diagnoses is produced.

UNDERDIAGNOSED   No decision is made, although M.G. gave a positive diagnostic decision.

TABLE 1. Performance of EMYCIN Series
on Transcript Set of 63 Patients

	Number of rules in knowledge base					
Decision category	21	34	49	58	67	78
Correct	46	51	65	75	73	77
Correct + other	8	8	3	3	6	2
Underdiagnosed	35	20	13	11	6	6
Overdiagnosed	6	10	10	10	8	8
Incorrect	5	10	10	1	6	6

OVERDIAGNOSED   A positive diagnosis is made, although M.G. found insufficient evidence for a diagnosis.

Table 1 shows the performance of the six systems on the transcript data. There is an apparent steady improvement in performance with increasing knowledge. With 21 rules diagnostic accuracy is 46%, and with 78 rules diagnostic accuracy is 77%. The 31% increase in accuracy is being primarily achieved by a 29% reduction in the number of cases that were underdiagnosed.

The performances of the six systems on the 100 new patients are strikingly different. Table 2 shows that there are two surprising features of these data. First, the increase in size of the knowledge base does not appear to have had any significant effect on the diagnostic accuracy of the developing expert system. Rather, instead of increasing accuracy at the expense of underdiagnosis, there appears to be merely a trading of false negative errors (underdiagnosis) for false positive errors (overdiagnosis and incorrects). In short, a quadrupling of the knowledge base has merely changed the trade-off criterion of the system; it has not improved its sensitivity. Figure 4 illustrates these trends graphically.

TABLE 2. Performance of EMYCIN Series
on the Test Set of 100 Patients

	Number of rules in knowledge base					
Decision category	21	34	49	58	67	78
Correct	68	64	66	62	64	69
Correct + other	1	2	2	5	3	3
Underdiagnosed	26	24	18	13	7	6
Overdiagnosed	3	6	7	14	17	13
Incorrect	2	4	7	6	9	9

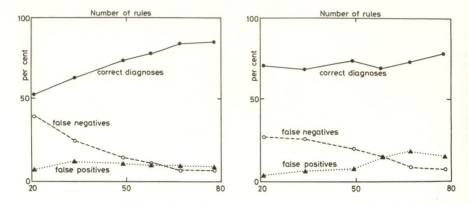

FIGURE 4. (a) Summary of data showing effect of increasing the size of the leukemia knowledge base on the proportion of correct and incorrect diagnoses, when tested on the transcript patients. Diagnostic accuracy is rising dramatically while false negative errors are correspondingly falling. (b) The same data but for the systems applied to a new series of 100 patient records. Apparently, the only effect of increasing the size of the knowledge base is to trade off false positive and false negative errors against each other. The proportion of correct diagnoses is hardly affected by the increase in knowledge base rules.

Second, it is also remarkable that the diagnostic accuracy of the first system, equipped with a mere 21 rules, was so high—68%. In fact, the rate was so high we suspected that our group of new patients was qualitatively different from the original transcript set.

Examination of the two series revealed differences in the frequency of different diagnoses. However, the most important difference was the frequency of cases that M.G. considered to be undiagnosable. As the systems grew, there was an increase in agreement with M.G. for those cases given a firm diagnosis, but no increase of agreement for those cases that M.G. decided were undiagnosable. Consequently, the overall

TABLE 3. Performance of EMYCIN Series
on the Transcript Set of 63 Patients after the Removal
of 9 Undiagnosable Cases

Decision category	Number of rules in knowledge base					
	21	34	49	58	67	78
Correct	44	55	70	81	78	82
Correct + other	9	9	4	4	7	2
Underdiagnosed	40	24	15	13	7	7
Incorrect	7	11	11	2	7	7

TABLE 4. Performance of EMYCIN Series
on the Test Set of 100 Patients after the Removal
of 37 Undiagnosable Cases

Decision category	Number of rules in knowledge base					
	21	34	49	58	67	78
Correct	53	52	57	59	70	73
Correct + other	5	3	3	8	5	5
Underdiagnosed	41	38	29	20	11	9
Incorrect	3	6	11	10	14	13

performance of the smaller systems was exaggerated by the undiagnosable cases that these systems will label "undiagnosable" owing to their limited expertise rather than a principled agreement with the expert. While there were only 9 undiagnosable cases in the transcript series, there were 37 such cases in the test series, and the score was therefore highly inflated.

To clarify this, the results were reanalyzed without the undiagnosable cases and are presented in Tables 3 and 4. These tables have dropped the "overdiagnosed" category. On the transcript series the effect is to enhance the trend seen before, in which correct diagnoses were increasingly achieved at the expense of errors of underdiagnosis. More important, on the remaining 67 patients of the test series an effect of adding knowledge is now apparent—an increase in diagnostic accuracy from 53% to 73%. The increase is again primarily due to a reduction in underdiagnosis, though there is also a fourfold increase in incorrect diagnoses.

5. ANALYSIS OF DISAGREEMENTS BETWEEN SYSTEM AND EXPERT

After we had put all the information extracted from the transcripts into the knowledge base, and we had taken account of the problem of the undiagnosable cases, we achieved an overall level of agreement with our expert of 73%. In other words, we still had a shortfall of 27%, which we considered to be unacceptably high for a practical system, and puzzling. The shortfall could be explained by several factors: (1) Protocol analysis is a poor technique that leads to a distorted or incomplete representation of a human expert's knowledge; (2) the transcript set is not representative of the range of leukemias; (3) all available knowledge has not been extracted from the protocols; (4) the expert is inconsistent owing to momentary error or other cause; (5) there may be incorrect estimates, or inappropriate use, of probabilities; (6) mistakes in formulating the rules can occur.

The transcription method certainly does not give a complete and accurate picture of the expert's knowledge. For example, while the method has provided ready access to knowledge that can be represented as simple rules and facts, the transcripts themselves gave no guidance about the higher-level structure of the task. The basic components of the task, defining the cell type and cell lineage, were implicit, not explicit, in the transcripts. Furthermore, the conditions governing when patients were considered to be "undiagnosable" were not spelled out. We assumed, by default, that if the diagnosis rules were not successful, then these were the conditions under which the patient was undiagnosable. It later turned out that, on the contrary, there are explicit conditions that determine when a case is undiagnosable. For example, a blood or bone marrow sample that is too small for a full set of tests, or test results that are in conflict, are circumstances that make a diagnosis inappropriate.

It is also clear that the particular set of 63 patients in the transcript set were not representative of the whole population of leukemia types— or even of the test series. At completion of the 58-rule system we carried out a case-by-case analysis of diagnostic errors on the test series. These were compiled into "error matrices" showing how frequently pairs of leukemias were confused. These matrices let us check whether there were systematic patterns of errors or whether they were randomly scattered. A systematic distribution would suggest that there were systematic weaknesses to be remedied with specifically targeted rules or facts. Unsystematic patterns would suggest a general lack of knowledge. The matrices showed that the system performed badly with a particular class of leukemias, the acute myeloid leukemias, and with certain rare types.

The problem of acquiring knowledge about rare cases cannot be easily remedied precisely because of the rarity of the cases—and asking the expert to consider imaginary cases would be dangerous, since the expert's own experience may be unrepresentative. On the question of the myeloid leukemias, at that time these were technically difficult to identify and were consequently not easily diagnosed without error. A new, highly specific myeloid test has since been introduced, and it was used for the test series.

The transcript series therefore was not representative of the range of leukemias, but little hint of this was to be found with this knowledge-acquisition method. Furthermore, it is also worth noting that "overfitting" of a diagnostic system to a particular training set is an artifact that is well known in statistics. Knowledge-based systems do not escape this problem.

Have we extracted all the knowledge possible from the transcripts? We do not know. Our method of identifying "useful" information in the protocols is strongly influenced by expert system technology, i.e., by the search for facts and rules. EMYCIN, a particular package with a particular knowledge representation, may also have influenced what we looked for in the transcripts. In our judgment the useful fragments of knowledge seemed obvious and rather distinct from the inevitable "padding" and insubstantial remarks in commentaries of this type. Although we believe in our judgment, it is completely intuitive and we cannot be dogmatic.

We are even less confident about knowledge that may be implicit, or distributed, in the structure of the protocols rather than concentrated in identifiable fragments. "Commonsense" knowledge, general problem-solving strategies, "deep" knowledge of the biological foundations of the domain, and so on, are likely examples of the sort of knowledge that a human expert may not think to mention (Shortliffe, 1984, personal communication). If there is significant information that we have missed, we shall have to wait for future elicitation techniques to reveal it.

Since the judgments of an expert are our gold standard, an important question is how much his judgment may vary, as human judgments do from time to time. We looked at this question directly by asking M.G. to diagnose two sets of 100 patients on two occasions, 1 month apart. Table 5 presents the results; apart from minor changes in the decision, the data show a significant inconsistency of about 8% in the two series. (It was generous of M.G. to expose himself in this way; it should be noted that a large part of his inconsistency may arise from the uncertainty inherent in a new field rather than simple errors.)

A large literature suggests that people are poor at numerical estimation of probability and do not naturally use such estimates in their own

TABLE 5. Results of M.G. Diagnosing the Same
Set of Patients on Two Occasions
Approximately 1 Month Apart

Series	Complete agreement	Minor inconsistency	Significant change
100/1	67	22	11
100/2	75	19	6

reasoning. We therefore considered whether the numerical certainty factors that had been added to the rules really contributed to the system's ability to emulate M.G. To check this, the certainty factors on version 5 of the system were changed to one of two values—either 1.0 if the rule made a logical (certain) influence or 0.5 otherwise. We were surprised to find that this produced about a 5% increase in agreement between the decisions of the system and those of M.G. (from 64% correct to 69% correct). Perhaps these parameters have not been reliably estimated, or M.G. does not use quantitative uncertainty in a way that resembles EMYCIN. Although the difference is not in the expected direction, it is not large and should not be overstated. However, it is consistent with the view that representations of uncertainty should reflect human understanding of uncertainty more closely (Cohen, 1984; Fox *et al.*, 1980; Fox, 1985).

Finally, the sixth knowledge base was found to contain a number of small errors in the implementation, e.g., rules referring to quantitative ranges like "between 20 and 30" and "between 30 and 40."

6. DISCUSSION

The leukemia diagnosis project is not complete. This chapter has not been concerned with system design, nor with final results, but with strategies for building expert systems. Leukemia was felt to be a small and simple enough field of application that it could be a model domain for examining knowledge-engineering methods. In fact, it turned out to be considerably more complex than we expected, but it has revealed some general points concerning the acquisition and formulation of knowledge bases.

The results suggest that protocols are a useful basis for starting to build a knowledge base. However, we believe it is limited because the protocols may not reflect some kinds of knowledge. They may not carry higher-order information about the structure of the task, notably the cell lineage/cell type distinction, and the strategy for dealing with "undiagnosable" cases. Nor did the protocols give any hint that the transcript set was unrepresentative of leukemia as a whole.

The sources of these errors were identified only by a systematic analysis of the error trends as the knowledge base grew. A case-by-case approach to debugging would have been insufficient.

Leukemia diagnosis is a small domain. Knowledge bases of several hundred to tens of thousands of facts and rules are anticipated in the future (e.g., Fox *et al.*, 1986). We may expect that the problems of knowledge acquisition will be proportionately greater.

The system has now been reimplemented by P. Alvey and M. Greaves. The new version has all minor implementation errors corrected; it contains an explicit method for making the decision "undiagnosable"; it incorporates additional knowledge to deal with new leukemia markers; it provides the qualifications on diagnoses ("possible," "compatible with") as well as the raw diagnoses; and it uses a logical, not numerical, representation of uncertainty. It is estimated that the level of agreement with M.G. on test series is now approaching 100%.

7. GUIDELINES SUMMARY

We do not claim that the acquisition of knowledge for building an expert system by the analysis of transcripts is wholly adequate either for expert systems in general or for diagnostic systems in particular. We chose this informal technique because we were not convinced that the alternative methods available were any better. Developments since the work was originally carried out suggest that other methods, such as induction, may have a role to play but they still leave many problems unsolved. Our purpose was to collect objective information about the acquisition of knowledge through systematic evaluation of system performance. We believe that this sort of evaluation is still important, and will continue to be important even as more powerful knowledge acquisition methods are developed.

The benefits of careful performance evaluation include the following:

1. Statements about rapid or slow progress in knowledge acquisition are meaningless in isolation. A large number of rules or facts in a knowledge base is of no consequence if the performance of the system cannot be shown to meet accepted performance criteria. Objective evaluation is necessary to show that these criteria are being met, or at least approached.
2. Progress is unlikely to be uniform with any complex application. Knowledge may be adequately clarified in some areas but prove to be weak or mistaken in others. Systematic evaluation, therefore, is important to identify the parts of the system where further development is required.
3. Many expert systems will require continuing maintenance and development to keep the knowledge base up to date. Systematic identification of those areas of the application where acceptable performance is easy or difficult to achieve is important for costing and managing the maintenance program. This process will

become increasingly crucial as knowledge bases become very large (e.g., Fox *et al.*, 1986).
4. Systematic evaluation is important for achieving credibility among skeptics, of whom there are still many.

We therefore recommend that at the project planning stage designers consider using the following evaluation techniques:

1. As a minimum, summary performance measures such as overall accuracy should be obtained. However, performance analysis should start with a clear statement of the performance criterion; an apparently high "hit rate" in decision making may be an illusion if it is accompanied by a high false positive rate, for example.
2. Unacceptable decisions or recommendations should be partitioned to reveal those parts of the knowledge base that are weak and what those weaknesses are. A technique we found to be helpful in this study was the compilation of an error matrix that indicated the frequencies with which decision A was confused with decision B and vice versa.
3. Since some errors are likely to be costly and others relatively innocuous, a desirable extension to the error matrix technique is the use of "error-cost matrices." Confusing decision A with decision B may be much less acceptable than the reverse error, for example. A cost matrix, in which each cell contains a measure of the cost of the error, can be combined with the error matrix by multiplying each value with the corresponding frequency measure, summing the values for all cells, and normalizing the result. This may yield a more realistic measure of system performance.
4. Since knowledge acquisition is progressive, evaluation should also be progressive. Performance data should be analyzed to reveal trends in performance, to guide the developers. In our study this showed up patterns that would simply not have been seen with "snapshot" evaluations.
5. The standard evaluation procedure of measuring performance prospectively should be used. High performance on the set of cases used in development does not mean, as we saw in this study, high performance on new cases.

7.1. Limits of the Methods Proposed

These methods may not be wholly suitable for all applications. More appropriate measures may need to be designed or adapted. It is important, however, that the system designer should be prepared to develop these measures, for the reasons given above. Limits of our techniques include the following:

1. The number of outcomes in a leukemia diagnosis problem is relatively small. In practice it may be difficult to obtain these measures easily for much larger applications. Automatic testing and collection of performance data may therefore be desirable.
2. Some of our techniques, like error matrices, are oriented toward the general tasks of "diagnosis" or "classification," where there is a definite criterion of an error. The next generation of expert systems that carry out constructive tasks like planning and design may require more sophisticated performance measures. For example, the degree to which the plan or design is optimal over a number of dimensions will be more appropriate and will therefore require different evaluation procedures. Knowledge-based systems may in due course require new evaluation concepts, but at this stage it seems unnecessary to reinvent the wheel; statistics, operations research, and other disciplines have developed perfectly good tools for evaluating and optimizing the expert systems that have appeared to date.

ACKNOWLEDGMENTS. EMYCIN was kindly made available for our work by Dr. B. Buchanan and Dr. E. H. Shortliffe of the Knowledge Systems Laboratory and the MYCIN Project of Stanford University. We are grateful to Ted Shortliffe, Richard Young, and Alison Kidd for extensive comments on earlier drafts of this paper; Peter Alvey contributed extensively to our interpretation of the results.

8. REFERENCES

Buchanan, B. G., and Shortliffe, E. H. (1984). *Rule-based expert systems*. Reading, Mass.: Addison-Wesley.

Cohen, P. R. (1984). *Heuristic reasoning about uncertainty: An artificial intelligence approach*. Boston, Mass.: Pitman.

Fox, J. (1984a). Expert systems: Towards a routine technology. Keynote lecture. *Proceedings of Medical Informatics Europe, Brussels* (pp. 19–23). Berlin: Springer-Verlag.

Fox, J. (1984b). Doubts about induction. *Bulletin of SPL Insight*. Abingdon, Oxford, England: SPL International.

Fox, J. (1985). Knowledge, decision making and uncertainty. In W. Gale and D. Pregibon (Eds.), *Proceedings of conference on AI and statistics, Bell Laboratories*. Reading, Mass.: Addison-Wesley.

Fox, J., Barber, D., and Bardhan, K. D. (1980). Alternatives to Bayes? A quantitative comparison with rule based diagnostic inference. *Methods of Information in Medicine*, 19(4), 210–215.

Fox, J., Duncan, T., Frost, D., Glowinski, A., Hajnal, S., and O'Neill, M. (1986). *Organising a large knowledge base: The Oxford System of Medicine*. Manuscript submitted for publication.

Hayes-Roth, F., Waterman, D. A., and Lenat, D. B. (1983). *Building expert systems*. Reading, Mass.: Addison-Wesley.

Mulsant, B., and Servan-Schreiber, D. (1984). Knowledge engineering: A daily activity on a hospital ward. *Computers and Biomedical Research, 17*, 71–91.

Shortliffe, E. H. (1976). *Computer-based medical consultations: MYCIN*. New York: Elsevier.

van Melle, W. (1980). *A domain independent system that aids in constructing knowledge-based consultation programs*. Doctoral dissertation, Computer Science Department, Stanford University (Stanford Reports No. STAN-CS-80-820).

Welbank, M. (1983). *A review of knowledge acquisition techniques for expert systems*. Martlesham Heath, Ipswich: Martlesham Consultancy Services, British Telecom Research Labs.

5

Knowledge Elicitation Involving Teachback Interviewing

LESLIE JOHNSON and NANCY E. JOHNSON

1. THE KNOWLEDGE ELICITATION PROCESS

Our knowledge elicitation technique has at its center a program of semi-structured interviews by a methodology based on conversation theory (Pask, 1974).

The first phase is a broad and shallow survey of domain experts and related personnel, as appropriate. This first phase is to prevent the interviewer prematurely fixing a perspective from which to analyze the expertise. Although the need for this preventative action has been long understood in educational research, only recently has it been brought to the attention of the knowledge-engineering community (Mittal and Dym, 1985).

The second phase is to undertake an investigation of the task structure and to narrow the focus of the analysis to a few experts with expertise that promises to yield an interesting analysis from a chosen perspective. During this phase one may narrow down to just one expert who is acknowledged by his peer group as having superior performance in the relevant task.

The third phase, not discussed in this chapter, is to further process the appropriateness and validity of the analysis by testing theoretical

LESLIE JOHNSON and NANCY E. JOHNSON • Department of Computer Science, Brunel University, Uxbridge, Middlesex UB8 3PH, England.

predictions made on the interviewer's understanding of the domain. This phase is carried out by contact with the initial community and a further, independent, population. We have used direct question format, statistical hypothesis testing, and other techniques in this phase.

Finally, we represent our understanding in knowledge representation schemes, but we also have material from which we can design training procedures and from which we can make recommendations for new working procedures in the domain of application.

The single most important facet of our work is that we treat interview data as *qualitative data* (N. E. Johnson, 1985; Silverman, 1985) to be analyzed from various perspectives. The analyses are expressed in a representation that will form the basis of an understanding sufficient to design a model of *competence* (L. Johnson, 1985a). Thus, our representational device, known as Systemic Grammar Networks (see Bliss *et al.*, 1983), acts as a *mediating* device between interview and knowledge representation schemes (N. E. Johnson, 1985). This device allows us to select, in a principled way, the knowledge representation scheme(s) that will best express the model of competence. The process of building Systemic Grammar Networks (see section 3) is the key stage in our attempts to represent the knowledge; it is here that we formally structure the expert's knowledge. Limitations on space do not permit a full account of how one encodes knowledge into a Systemic Grammar Network, but a full understanding of our methodology cannot be had without it. We strongly advise the reader to turn to the guidance in Bliss *et al.* (1983).

1.1. THEORETICAL STANCE

Our theoretical stance is that in expert systems design we need to model more than "good as expert" *performance;* rather we need to model *competence* (L. Johnson, 1985a). We are, therefore, most interested in ways of capturing the expert's *conceptual* structure, not just his procedural skills. This statement might appear noncontroversial, but even the most cursory glance at current systems (see Johnson and Keravnou, 1985) reveals that only very recently have serious attempts been made to model concepts rather than procedures. Modeling competence in an expert system gives new effectiveness and acceptability (L. Johnson, 1985b; Murdoch, 1985).

Insight into strategies and knowledge structures may be gained by examining the dialogue structure between expert and knowledge eliciter (provided that the eliciter's questions are guided by appropriate theoretical constructs). Evidence for the interdependence between the domain strategies and structure and the dialogue structure is provided through various attempts (Kassirer *et al.*, 1982). For example, Clancey (1985) traces backward through the explanations of the reasoning processes that triggered the questions that an expert raised in his or her activities. Explanations are a linguistic phenomenon, that is, not a motor response or observable performance. Thus, we are led to using an elicitation technique that is a natural forum for explanations—language itself. Since we are dealing with expert's knowledge, which is characteristically complex and esoteric, we need a versatile and highly expressive medium. Language, as our most cognitively sophisticated tool, is an obvious choice and is at its most flexible in a personal interview. Thus, we maintain that a flexible interview technique like ours is a viable tool for eliciting the *global* picture of an expert's knowledge necessary for constructing credible expert systems.

1.2. CONVERSATION THEORY

Conversation theory has no obvious connection with what we would ordinarily call conversation. For our purpose here we must take the terms to be stipulatively defined by Pask's work and not import too much of the terms' common meaning into our interpretation. Our description of conversation theory is but a gesture toward the original. We suggest that further reference first be made to Ogborn and Johnson (1984) and then reference be made to the original source (say, Pask, 1974).

Conversation theory is partially concerned (and here wholly concerned) with the notions of concepts and understanding as entities made public or objective by an interaction between participants. From this perspective, for an interview to take place in which A (the analyst) attempts to find out what E (the expert) knows, E must agree to be a participant in the role of interviewee. A and E must contract to play the same game. They must decide on the area of discussion (the domain) and on the medium of conversation (verbal, written, or doing something). The expert establishes the content of the domain. This content is expressed in terms of "relations," a very general term, which may be (1) for the domain of typing: the relations of the alphabet to their positions on the keyboard; (2) for the domain of sums: "Multiplication is a type of sum" or "All sums have answers"; (3) for the domain of electronics: This arrangement of four pass gates is a barrel shifter.

Our analysis of an interaction, as dictated by conversation theory, is at two levels: Level 0 and Level 1 (L_0, L_1).

At Level 0 we have procedures that bring about a specified relation.

Notice that this is not a category or class definition. So when E is asked, "What's this multiplication thing all about?" he may describe a procedure for multiplying two numbers, and this procedure is evidence for his having the concept of multiplication. Other questions that elicit the explication of L_0 procedures as answers are: How do you do multiplication sums? Why did you do that (string of acts)? L_0 answers are often explanations of how to do an algorithm.

At Level 1 we have the method for the reconstruction of L_0 procedures. For example, how one remembers or recollects how to do a procedure is an L_1 activity. Examples of questions that tend to elicit L_1 activity are: How do you know multiplication always works? What do you need to know to be able to do it? How do you remember what to do? How would you teach a novice how to do it? Do you know any equivalent methods? Why can you trust that method/system? L_1 answers are often explanations of why algorithms work. They are explanations of explanations.

Notice that these L_1 questions are sufficiently general in form to be usable in any domain of application where some sort of procedure or chain of activities is present. In the field one would tie the L_1 question to a specific, usually previously discussed, description of human acts. For example, in algorithmic problem-solving activities, "Why does that method work?" and for VLSI design, "Why can you trust a SPICE simulation?"

In a conversation E will describe a procedure to A. A will teach it back to E in E's terms and to E's satisfaction. When they agree that A is doing the procedure E's way, then it can be said that A and E share the same concept. This "teachback" procedure is a checking device where E is the final judge. Notice that A and E do not necessarily have the same private thought processes. They just agree that the same thing has been done. Then A asks E to give an L_1 explanation of how he reconstructed that concept and the teachback procedure continues until E is satisfied with A's version. Then we can say that A has understood E. Briefly then: at L_0 procedures define concepts, which, through Teachback, lead to shared concepts; at L_1 reconstructions define "memories," which, through teachback, lead to understanding.

Having established understanding of a particular relation, E chooses another to discuss. To maintain the participant–expert ethos, any topic to be discussed must originate from E. The minimal criterion for acceptance is that E must be able to specify at least one link between this topic and some other. A must name the topics consistently in terms that E accepts or at least the terms and links must be translated into a form that E can and does appreciate; otherwise the teachback procedure will founder on a confusion of terms.

2. CASE STUDIES

We have used teachback interviewing in two areas. The first was an investigation of children's arithmetic knowledge (N. E. Johnson, 1983) and the second is a current investigation of VLSI designer's knowledge (SERC Project No. GR/C/688.3.5, 1987).

2.1. WHY USE TEACHBACK INTERVIEWING?

In the first study of children's arithmetic knowledge the teachback style of interviewing was chosen as the main research tool, with a standardized mathematics test providing some background information. There were three areas of concern: complexity, private and public knowledge, and the nature of explanation. Of course, these areas are of such general concern as to be relevant to any knowledge engineer working with an expert in the domain under investigation.

Complexity. It was assumed that children's ideas of arithmetic were complex and systematic. To explore those ideas required a flexible research tool and a period of sustained investigation. A 2-hour single interview, apart from exhausting the participants, gives very little opportunity to explore a system of knowledge. Teachback in operation brings the expert's view of the domain complexity into view.

Private and Public Knowledge. Pask's conversation theory is all about the action of making ideas and knowledge public whether they be procedural, declarative, meta, or "A.N. Other" type knowledge.

Nature of Explanation. It is unreasonable to expect a child (or even an adult) to give a full explanation of an abstract, albeit familiar, topic in a few words. An explanation emerges only during extended discussion. This quality of conversation, a given explanation by a participant, is what is not captured by a single question-and-answer couplet.

The most marked feature of the study with 12-year-olds was that the investigator held a well-established view of the nature of arithmetic but was aiming *not* to view the child's version through the adult version. Hence, the simple, but in that circumstance novel, idea of treating the child as an expert with esoteric, complex, and systematic knowledge. This idea dovetailed neatly with the conversational notion of participant interviewing rather than standard interrogator–respondent interviewing.

In the study of VLSI design, we have a genuine community of experts with a definitive body of esoteric knowledge, whose work practices are only partially documented. The concerns of complexity, private and public knowledge, and the problems of explanation still apply. VLSI design is complex and systematic, not completely intuitive, and designers *do* it rather than talk about it. The investigation into their expertise is a test bed for teachback methodology. The view is that, if teachback interviewing is a "good" elicitation technique, then it should be seen to work in a situation where the interviewer is naive. If we take this view seriously, then checking the veracity of our versions of VLSI design with a larger community of experts should be a major concern. In this respect we take a lead from social science research by building a period of checking for validity into the main body of the research. However, we have chosen this area as a test bed because the knowledge elicited is of real interest to the community of experts. One such interest arises from the obvious commitment to expensive man and machine power in VLSI, and management thus needs to reflect upon how those resources are used. On top of this there is a very high degree of staff mobility in electronic systems design, and lack of continuity on projects is proving to be an important consideration. We believe that teachback methodology and representation through Systemic Networks could be a valuable tool in staff debriefing and training. In addition, we are concerned to provide a good methodology for the building of expert systems and knowledge-based aids. (Knowledge elicitation cannot be separated from other issues in the design of these systems. For details, see Weiss and Kulikowski, 1984.)

2.2. ARITHMETIC STUDY

The "expert" community were eight 12-year-old children in a comprehensive school in an outer London borough. A pair of children were allocated a 3-week slot and each of the pair gave six interviews of about half an hour's length. Interviews were conducted before school in the morning in a quiet room in the sixth-form block. Tape recordings of the interview were transcribed immediately after the interviews so that graphical and indexed prose summaries could be made before returning for the next interview. The child was told that the investigator was interested in "how children did math," which was known to sometimes differ from the teacher's version, and "how to draw pictures of what children knew." (This was much closer to the truth than a normal investigation into children's cognitive processes.) They were told they would not be set problems in the interviews and would be helped to teach the interviewer what they knew about "sums." The first interview generated a collection of topics to discuss. The child elaborated upon a chosen subset of these topics on subsequent occasions. In a typical set of six interviews we would use the *first interview* to give an introduction to interview procedure, to elicit a list of words considered to be "important in sums," and to sort those words into natural groups. This provided a first summary and a basis for further work. For example, a child might say that all sums need two numbers, a sign and an answer. In the later sessions he could fill out the notions of number, sign, and answer. In the *second interview* the child was shown how the first summary was constructed from the list of words and the transcript. The child chose a topic from the summary to develop (usually numbers and their properties or an arithmetic algorithm). This interview is considered to be crucial in demonstrating commitment to the expert done through sharing the research process and allowing choice of topic to be discussed. During the *third, fourth,* and *fifth interviews* summaries of previous interviews were checked and another topic was chosen and developed. The *sixth* interview was used to check the final summary of all elicited knowledge (the child was given a copy).

It was usually possible to have collected information about the following areas: numbers, their types and properties; an arithmetic operation: how to do it and its properties; other objects in sums (very large and very small numbers); other numerical systems; other algebraic expressions; and other operations in less detail. Within each area information was elicited on the salient features as the child saw them. These were names, necessary features, and criteria for identifying bona fide examples as well as the more straightforward procedural descriptions. The following questions, generated prior to the interview, were most commonly asked. How do you do X? Can you show me which of these are all right (= reasonable and acceptable examples of X)? Can you tell me why that one (an unreasonable and unacceptable example of X) is strange? What do you need to be able to do X? How do you know that is right? How do you know that works? Are any of these the same in any way? Can you think back to when you learned X? Did you use any special things (apparatus, tools, incidents, etc.)?

When the child gave a description of a procedure or some piece of content, the interviewer taught it back to the child using the child's terminology, seeking confirmation of whether or not they were doing it the same way. If the child disagreed, the investigator asked the child for further information or instruction, and the cycle of teach and teachback was repeated until the child was satisfied that the investigator was doing the same thing. During this teachback cycle the child will typically display behavior that suggests uncertainty or lack of confidence. It is at this point that the interviewer needs to proceed very gently with teachback in order to elicit the *child's* knowledge and not just superimpose a "correct" viewpoint. In our experience, the children talked at length only on topics of which they were confident, yet still prevaricated or changed their minds during the early parts of the elicitation process. We took this to be a natural part of bringing out ideas in verbal form. With due care and attention to interviewing procedure it was never a permanent stumbling block. In general, hesitation and lack of clarity can be indications that the expert's view diverges from orthodoxy. The dialogue here may be marked as a possible returning place for investigation; however, as teachback progresses it may develop that returning is not necessary.

The conversation then changed levels whereby the child was asked about the procedure or content. Questions about how to remember how to do a procedure and why it was correct became appropriate at this stage. Again the child was required to approve or veto the interviewer's understanding of his own knowledge. The questions listed above therefore had a double function. They were start-up questions to get the discussion going or allow the child out of a psychologically oppressive situation, and they were questions designed to elicit a level of informal but powerful knowledge about sums.

2.2.1. Analyzing Data

Summaries made after interviews were of two forms: an idiosyncratic, graphical nodes-and-arrows-type summary (use your own favorite) and an indexed list of near-verbatim comments. Both summaries stayed close to the original data. Some 3 months later the collection of data was analyzed using two representation schemes: First, the children's knowledge was written in frames based on Rissland Michener's work on the structure of mathematical knowledge (Rissland Michener, 1978); second, more interestingly, the same verbal data were analyzed using Systemic Grammar Networks (see section 3 in this chapter and Chapter 3 in Bliss *et al.*, 1983).

2.2.2. Results

From the arithmetic study we have eight packages of children's ideas of sums in the form of SGNs, frames, summaries, indexed notes, and the interview transcripts. Through teachback we were reasonably sure that we had "expert-approved" versions of the children's knowledge. For example, we had, as a rule of thumb, that the child could not be considered to be behaving as an expert until he or she had either corrected the interviewer or asked for clarification at least twice. It was clear that the children had been willing volunteers. The 8 children turned up regularly and punctually, in their own time, and seemed fascinated by the summaries of their knowledge. A ninth, not particularly assertive, child withdrew after the second interview—itself evidence of genuine volunteer status. All that was left was to make sure that this cosy and intimate experience had not degenerated into a subtle but fictional collection of ideas about sums. We therefore asked 113 similarly placed children to comment on some 60 statements, most taken verbatim from transcripts. To give some idea of the success of the elicitation technique, we quote a small result in that 86% of the children were able to reject less than 30% of the statements as meaningless and agreed substantially with the remainder. Furthermore, it was felt that, if the interviewer really did know the children's "theories," she should be able to predict their performance. So the investigator, after the interviews were completed, made a blind prediction of the performance of the 8 children in a standard pencil-and-paper maths test done by the whole class of 12-year-olds. There was a gross overall success rate of 70%. (More detail of the analyses conducted can be found in N. E. Johnson, 1983.)

2.3. VLSI Design Study

The naive, but science-trained, investigator began with a few weeks' familiarization with basic electronics and digital design to gain at least some vocabulary. The expert community was 10 custom and semi-custom VLSI designers in two U.K. companies. Each interview was less than 1 hour, and there were batches of six with an optional seventh for demonstration of CAD systems or work stations. As in the previous study, we started with a question designed to elicit topics for discussion. A typical example was something like "Imagine walking into a bookshop and discovering the book on VLSI design you wish you had had when you started working—what sorts of things are in it?"

Designers are asked to group topics in any way that seems appropriate to them. From their response, the eliciter constructs particular questions of the general L_0 and L_1 type. These questions are prompts, not probes. So far we have used variations on these questions. For L_0: What does X device (a barrel shifter) look like at Y level (transistor level)? When do you document this part of the design? What sort of diagram is appropriate here? Is this a good example of an X (memory cell)? For L_1: How do you know you can trust that algorithm/simulation? Is this part of the job like any other job outside electronic engineering? What do you need to know to be able to do that? How do you know when to stop? Where/How did you learn this?

To date there is a collection of statements made on some 40 topics ranging from trade-offs in the design process, how to choose an architecture, and floor planning, right down to how to lay out an operational amplifier or barrel shifter at transistor level. It is too early to measure the success of the teachback methodology in this study, but of the interviews done, none has been canceled; it is the *interviewer* who has been forced to call the interviews to a halt through fatigue; and all of the partial summaries have been revised and approved by the designers. It is worth noting that, like the children, the designers are very interested in the summaries made. These and the first interview transcript act as a very good focus for the discussion as well as providing a between-interviews teachback aid.

Teachback in the children's interviews often amounted to actually doing a calculation on paper. In the VLSI study teachback takes a more relaxed form. It can be a repeating back of the described procedure, but since this can degenerate into two mutually irritating monologues, it was found necessary to think of ways to display understanding without repeating. Three auxiliary methods are often used: (1) The investigator summarizes on the spot, distinguishing between levels of electronic detail and a conceptual level; (2) the investigator anticipates a form of expression or provides an alternative expression; (3) the investigator "chimes in" toward the end of a sentence. These alone are not sufficient evidence for satisfactory teachback, but with the between-interviews summaries as backup, the expert's approval is gained without frustrating the expert in his task of putting abstractions into words.

2.3.1. Results

It is premature to quote results in this study. However, it is clear that the VLSI designers are willing to take part in the experiment although there is no tangible stick or carrot involved. In short, they like being participants! We believe it is the humanity of this interview procedure, with its lack of experimental subterfuge and the close interest taken in the expert's knowledge, that is so appealing! Six interviews cannot exhaust the knowledge available, but neither has it exhausted the expert's patience and interest.

We are using the SGN notation in parts of the interview to reflect back the expert's knowledge with a view to identifying areas of knowledge that could be elicited through the structure of the network in a more efficient machine-codable form. One of the results of the project will be an analysis of how and where SGNs may be appropriate for eliciting knowledge directly.

3. MEDIATING REPRESENTATION—SGN

Systemic Grammar Networks (SGNs) are the representation scheme used by linguists to formalize their functional approach to grammar. Systemic Grammar Networks provide an empty structure into which a chosen domain of knowledge may be fit. The "content-free" nature of networks is the most appealing feature in the search for ways of representing qualitative data emanating from interview transcripts.

Like other associative networks, a Systemic Grammar Network is a graph composed of nodes joined by links. Unlike other associative networks, the nodes are invented by the analyst but suggested by the *data*, not, as has normally been the case in knowledge representation, by some epistemological scheme underpinning the formalism. For an example we can draw upon Bliss *et al.* (1983, p. 180). There it is shown that "Socrates is a man" is represented as in Figure 1. It can be seen that the network has essentially just one link, an and/or pointer denoted by curly/straight brackets. Thus, in analysis with SGNs everything has to go into the terms, including all the relations. (In this way one gets the neutrality that is desirable.) The nodes are of three types: one that fur-

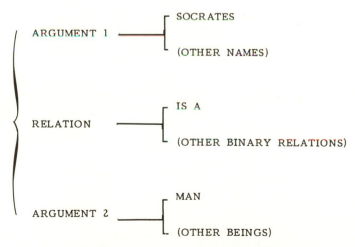

FIGURE 1. "Socrates is a man" expressed in SGN form.

ther describes a prior term, one that shows what types may be selected, and one that shows the aspects out of which a description falling under the term should be constructed.

There are other notions associated with the notation: a recursion symbol allowing optional choice to repeat a node (useful for unusual combinations of features); a conditional link, used in conjunction with entry conditions, allows selected combinations of distinctions to be collected together for the purpose of developing a new area of the domain (see Bliss *et al.*, 1983).

The exercise of building SGNs has demonstrated that it is possible to represent idiosyncratic and messy knowledge, embedded in several pages of transcript, in a one page, purpose-built structure without throwing out the individual flavor of the original source (Figure 2).

Figure 2 is a section of an SGN developed to characterize design decisions as described by one VLSI designer. This designer spontaneously described why certain decisions were made during a long and fluent dialogue about the nature of graphical documentation of chip designs. (Such efficient knowledge elicitation, collecting on two topics at once, is not rare and commonly induces panic in the interviewer!) Figure 2 was built up from the extremities toward the center of the page but is to be "read" from left to right, as follows: One group of strategies involved in VLSI design comprises the OPTIMIZING STRATEGIES. These have two (cooccurring) aspects, a TYPE and a DOMAIN. The three TYPES are MAXIMIZING strategies, CONVENIENCE strategies, and SAFETY strategies. The DOMAIN has two aspects. One has to do with the design *per se* (the DESIGN aspect) and the other with the amount of EFFORT involved. Further nodes on the left-hand side give successively more detailed descriptions of their "parent" nodes. Here we show only the bald shorthand forms to give an indication of the kind of relationship between an SGN and knowledge embedded in a conversion. In practice one would have a glossary of terms.

The building of networks thus gives us two advantages: (1) Deciding what to put in and how to name a node is an excellent way of doing what social scientists call "getting to know your data" or "forming data-driven concepts." This seems to be exactly the problem a knowledge engineer faces during knowledge elicitation! (2) Communicating an individual's knowledge to another or comparing individuals' knowledge through comparing transcripts are tortuous tasks that seductively lead the analyst into expressing trivial aspects of an expert's knowledge in the form of anecdotes or simple classification systems. Knowledge engineers need a representation for handling complex information that is transparent to the author and other members of the expert system build-

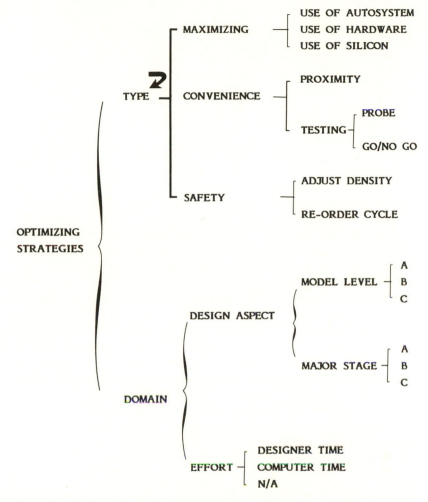

FIGURE 2. Part of an SGN to characterize the nature of design decisions in VLSI.

ing team. SGNs look like a good candidate for this mediating representation between verbal data and computer program.

4. DISCUSSION

The VLSI project has a suite of knowledge-elicitation techniques that form a complete methodology. Teachback interviewing and writing

Systemic Grammar Networks are two of the central techniques. We will also add techniques extant in systems analysis—e.g., task analysis and tailored techniques for checking our conceptions with a wider field (probably a questionnaire with statistical analysis). However, if one were to pick up teachback interviewing as a sole elicitation technique, then practical problems of completeness and viability would soon arise. We discuss these now as a warning.

4.1. TEACHBACK AS A COMPLETE METHODOLOGY

We see the actual elicitation of knowledge and the initial analysis/conceptualization/description of that knowledge in a form communicable to a third party *all* as part of the elicitation technique. We use teachback to generate a fund of ideas, facts, and procedures in the form of an interview transcript. But the transcript does not "talk" of its own volition. It is the interviewer's interpretation (for us in terms of SGNs) that conveys content. Our contribution to this standard difficulty in knowledge elicitation is to have developed a more rigorous means of collecting knowledge with teachback and a more expressive means of packaging it for internal communication in SGNs. We feel we have reasonable empirical grounds for trusting our intuitions in the results quoted in 2.2.2. and the anecdotal information in 2.3.1. We do feel that it is essential to do further quantitative tests to check the validity and reliability of the knowledge elicited. Teachback is a ready-made checking device by definition, but our thoughts often do wander to social science and systems analysis techniques of investigation! We cannot stress too strongly that eliciting knowledge is social science research, not merely uncovering self-evident "data."

Although we claim to have a better chance than most of eliciting a fair account of an expert's knowledge, this does not excuse us from seeking to establish the veracity of our conclusions by means other than writing a suite of programs. In simple terms, we are saying that realizing the knowledge in an expert system does not guarantee that the knowledge is appropriate or accurate for a *community* of experts. Checking procedures beyond the original informant should be completed by the knowledge engineer at least logically prior to machine implementation. So, teachback methodology is not a complete elicitation technique. Neither is it an all-purpose one! We can do a deep trawl of an expert's knowledge in a few hours. We can capture details and the essence, flavor, or overall shape of an expert's knowledge through a combination of teachback and SGN writing. We might here have used terms like *metaknowledge, strategic knowledge,* and *heuristics* but for their acquired technical usage in expert systems. However, they are *semantically* appropriate in this case. But there are circumstances when a conversational approach is simply long-winded. At the moment in the VLSI study we are looking for areas to sidetrack into a more straightforward elicitation method. For example, we could envisage using standard teachback methodology to generate relevant characteristics or features of the domain, constructing a patchy network, and "reading" it to generate questions that require specific responses (yes/no or more detail).

In terms of conducting interviews it is well nigh impossible to understand a description of a manual skill or perceptual task on a piece of equipment without videotape. On the surface, then, teachback is not the best way to capture such knowledge. The verbal to-ing and fro-ing, if it were to work, would result in a wonderfully explicit description! However, it is probably too frustrating for all concerned to insist on verbal explicitness alone. The dialogue is too context-bound to make for a perspicuous transcription. In this situation ("you press this and this happens") it would be wiser to do teachback with visual backup or introduce another method.

4.2. Teachback Interviewing as a Viable Technique

The characteristics of teachback as the participant interviewing with access to products of the interview and the expert controlling the interview lead the investigator into good interviewing practices in the following ways:

1. The investigator has to create and maintain a social situation that, if it fails, invalidates his data. He therefore takes care not to intimidate the expert.

2. The principle of sharing knowledge keeps the expert's interest so that it is an enjoyable experience. The expert's knowledge is valued for itself; no judgment is passed on it.

3. Unfortunately, the nonjudgmental aspect and the lack of direction by the interviewer can leave the interviewee drifting. The mechanics of teachback and demonstrating how summaries are constructed gives the expert an anchor and *aide-mémoire* for his thoughts.

4. The difficulty the naive investigator has in absorbing material leads to considerable mental fatigue. This forces the investigator to keep the interviews short. This ensures that the investigator does not become a nuisance or a bore, but it is not an elicitation technique for the fainthearted investigator.

5. Not only does transcribing and partially analyzing tapes between interviews lead to clearer understanding during the interview sessions, it also breaks the transcription task (or the reading of the prepared transcription) into manageable pieces. Full transcription must be done in order that the interviewer make the most of the experts offerings at the time and to allow successive passes at the data. After all, it is a monstrously tedious task to transcribe a pile of tapes when all the interviews are completed (1 hour of tape = 6 hours of transcription). So tedious is it that most would revert to brief note taking or picking out what seem, at the time, to be key concepts, thus not utilizing the full strength of interviewing.

6. Using an interview technique that focusses on levels of knowledge and not just on topics allows the interviewer to employ other interview techniques locally without taking on board the full force of the theory of other approaches. For example, when setting up a primary group of topics to discuss, we can elicit connections between topics by using the repertory grid technique of asking for similarities and differences on a bipolar dimension (Shaw and Gaines, Chapter 6, this volume). We would not wish to limit the interviewee to expressing all his varied knowledge in such a limited framework but it can be slotted in and around our L_0 and L_1 questions. Also, a problem-solving situation will arise naturally when experts give examples of things that went wrong. The interviewer, by questioning the interviewee on his problem solving, may easily prejudice the participant relationship. But by exploiting teachback in its most basic sense he can retrieve the situation.

5. GUIDELINES SUMMARY

5.1. Strengths

- Designed to elicit global and specific structures.
- Produces an *expert's* conception minimally prejudiced with respect to the knowledge engineer's preconceptions about the domain.
- Produces an expert authenticated fund of data that can be analyzed and represented in several ways.
- A nonpsychological, nonjudgmental technique enjoyed by experts.
- Encourages good interview practice (valuing expert, efficient use of expert's time, etc.).

- Allows eclectic use of other techniques for special purposes.
- In conjunction with SGNs, produces a communicable description of the knowledge before machine implementation.

5.2. WEAKNESSES

- Not a strongly structured technique, so requires general interview training (as do all interview techniques).
- Heavy cognitive load on the investigator, so not recommended for the fainthearted or infirm.
- Interviews are cumulative with transcription in between, so occupies a large slice of investigator's time.
- Not universally applicable; we specifically exclude perceptual skills and recommend care with motor skills.

5.3. RULES OF THUMB

- Think "participants," not interrogator/respondent.
- Create a list of L_0 and L_1 questions.
- Think of a couple of ways to generate a list of possible topics to discuss.
- Establish a "contract" at the beginning of the interviews. Discuss volunteer status, medium in which to work, domain to be discussed.
- Tell the interviewee he is to teach the naive investigator what he knows, although the investigator is not going to become an expert.
- During interviews give control of discussion to interviewee by allowing him/her to choose topics and order of discussion and whether or not he/she requires prompts.
- Summarize and teachback during interviews (adapting teachback for individual).
- Transcribe and summarize between interviews.
- Give the interviewee a copy of the first transcription and ask for comments (warning that transcribed speech does not have the elegance of prose!).
- Encourage the interviewee to alter or add to summaries.
- Use the last interview to check the products of interviews one to five.
- Keep all notes and diagrams.
- Keep interviews short (less than 1 hour).

6. REFERENCES

Bliss, J., Monk, M., and Ogborn, J. M. (1983). *Qualitative data analysis for educational research: A guide to the use of systemic networks.* London: Croom Helm.

Clancey, W. J. (1985). Acquiring, representing and evaluating a competence model of diagnostic strategy. In M. T. H. Chi, R. Glaser, and M. Farr (Eds.), *The nature of expertise.* Columbus, Ohio: National Center for Research on Vocational Education.

Johnson, L. (1985a). The need for competence models in the design of expert systems. *International Journal in Systems Research and Information Science, 1,* 23–36.

Johnson, L. (1985b). Organising a findings base for use in a competent automated diagnostician. *International Journal in Systems Research and Information Science, 1*(2), 91–112.

Johnson, L., and Keravnou, E. T. (1985). *Expert systems technology: A guide.* London: Abacus Press.

Johnson, N. E. (1983). *Elicitation and representation of children's arithmetic knowledge.* Doctoral dissertation, Chelsea College, University of London.

Johnson, N. E. (1985). Varieties of representation in eliciting and representing knowledge for IKBS. *International Journal in Systems Research and Information Science, 1*(2), 69–90.

Kassirer, J. P., Kuipers, B. J., and Gorry, G. A. (1982). Toward a theory of clinical expertise. *American Journal of Medicine, 73,* 251–259.

Mittal, S., and Dym, C. L. (1985). Knowledge acquisition from multiple experts. *AI Magazine, Summer,* 32–37.

Murdoch, S. T. (1985). Intelligent databases for expert systems. *International Journal in Systems Research and Information Science, 1*(3), 145–162.

Ogborn, J. M., and Johnson, L. (1984). Conversation theory. *Kybernetes, 13,* 177–181. ss

Pask, G. (1974). *Conversation, cognition and learning: A cybernetic theory and methodology.* London: Elsevier.

Rissland Michener, E. (1978). Understanding understanding mathematics. *Cognitive Science, 2*(4), 361–383.

SERC Project. (1987). *Knowledge transfer in the context of electronic systems design,* GR/C/6883.5. Uxbridge: Department of Electrical Engineering, Brunel University.

Silverman, D. (1985). *Qualitative methodology and sociology.* Brookfield, Vt.: Gower.

Weiss, S. M., and Kulikowski, C. A. (1984). *A practical guide to designing expert systems.* London: Rowman and Allenheld.

6

An Interactive Knowledge-Elicitation Technique Using Personal Construct Technology

MILDRED L. G. SHAW and BRIAN R. GAINES

1. KNOWLEDGE ENGINEERING

The initial success of expert system (ES) developments (Gevarter, 1983; Michie, 1979; Reitman, 1984) and the development of a number of reasonably domain-independent software support systems for the encoding and application of knowledge (Hayes-Roth *et al.*, 1983) have opened up the possibility of widespread usage of ESs. In particular, the Japanese Fifth Generation Computing System (FGCS) development program (Gaines, 1984; Moto-oka, 1982) assumes this will happen and is targeted on knowledge processing rather than information processing. However, what Feigenbaum (1980) terms *knowledge engineering*, the reduction of a large body of knowledge to a precise set of facts and rules, has already become a major bottleneck impeding the application of ESs in new domains. We need to understand more about the nature of expertise in itself (Hawkins, 1983) and to be able to apply this knowledge to the elicitation of expertise in specific domains.

MILDRED L. G. SHAW and BRIAN R. GAINES • Department of Computer Science, University of Calgary, Calgary, Alberta, Canada T2N 1N4.

The problems of knowledge engineering have been stated clearly:

> Knowledge acquisition is a bottleneck in the construction of expert systems. The knowledge engineer's job is to act as a go-between to help an expert build a system. Since the knowledge engineer has far less knowledge of the domain than the expert, however, communication problems impede the process of transferring expertise into a program. The vocabulary initially used by the expert to talk about the domain with a novice is often inadequate for problem-solving; thus the knowledge engineer and expert must work together to extend and refine it. One of the most difficult aspects of the knowledge engineer's task is helping the expert to structure the domain knowledge, to identify and formalize the domain concepts. (Hayes-Roth *et al.*, 1983).

The problem of knowledge elicitation from a skilled person is well known in the literature of psychology. Bainbridge (1979) has reviewed the difficulties of verbal debriefing and notes that there is no necessary correlation between verbal reports and mental behavior, and that many psychologists feel strongly that verbal data are useless. However, this remark must be taken in the context of experimental psychologists working within a positivist, behavioral paradigm. Other schools of psychology see the problem not as methodological but as psychological and resulting from cognitive defenses that impede internal communication for a variety of reasons (Freud, 1914; Rogers, 1967). Clinical psychologists in particular have developed techniques for making use of verbal interaction to identify underlying cognitive processes, for example, through structured interviewing techniques. These can be used to bypass cognitive defenses, including those resulting from automization of skilled behavior. Welbank (1983) has reviewed many of these techniques in the context of knowledge engineering.

This chapter is concerned with interactive computer aids to the knowledge engineer based on Kelly's (1955) Personal Construct Psychology (PCP), which uses a model of the person that has strong systemic and psychological foundations (Gaines and Shaw, 1981a; Mancuso and Adams-Webber, 1982; Shaw and Gaines, 1981a, 1981c, 1985). PCP provides a model of human knowledge representation, acquisition, and processing that has been made operational through computer programs for interactive knowledge elicitation (Shaw, 1980, 1982). These may be used in developing the expert's vocabulary and in encoding aspects of his reasoning for a rule-based system. The expert interacts with a program (Shaw and Gaines, 1981b, 1984) that encourages him to make clear the distinctions he uses in applying his expertise. This helps him to structure his knowledge and identify and formalize his concepts. The methodology may also be used in a teaching mode in order to enable others to come to use the expert's vocabulary in the same way as he does. Some experiments have been described (Shaw and Gaines, 1983a) to validate the use of the methodology in this way by reconstructing the basic distinctions used in the Business Information Analysis and Integration Technique (BIAIT) used to determine the accounting needs of a company (Carlson, 1979; Sowa, 1984).

2. PERSONAL CONSTRUCT PSYCHOLOGY

Kelly developed a systemic theory of human cognition based on the single primitive of a *construct*, or dichotomous distinction. For an individual, constructs are "transparent templets which he creates and then attempts to fit over the realities of which the world is composed" (Kelly, 1955). He proposes that all of human activity can be seen as a process of anticipating the future by construing the replication of events: "Constructs are used for predictions of things to come, and the world keeps rolling on and revealing these predictions to be either correct or misleading. This fact provides a basis for the revision of constructs and, eventually, of whole construct systems" (Kelly, 1955). Hence, his psychological model of man is strongly epistemological and concerned with the way in which man models his experience and uses this model to anticipate the future. The anticipation may be passive, as in prediction, or active, as in action.

Kelly developed his theory in the context of clinical psychology and hence was concerned to have techniques that used it to bypass cognitive defenses and elicit the construct systems underlying behavior. This is precisely the problem of knowledge engineering noted above. His *repertory grid* (Shaw, 1980) is a way of representing personal constructs as a set of distinctions made about elements relevant to the problem domain. In clinical psychology this domain will often be personal relationships, and the elements may be family members and friends. In the development of ESs the elements will be key entities in the problem domain, such as oil-well sites or business transactions. Repertory grids have been widely used in clinical psychology (Shepherd and Watson, 1982), to study processes of knowledge acquisition in education (Pope and Shaw, 1981), and to study decision making by individuals and groups in management (Shaw, 1980). PLANET (Shaw, 1982) is an integrated suite of programs that operationalizes Kelly's work and may be used for the interactive elicitation and analysis of repertory grids. These programs have been widely used internationally in clinical psychology, education, and management studies (Shaw, 1981), and the present chapter describes their application to knowledge engineering for ESs.

Kelly's PCP is important because it develops a complete psychology of both the normal and the abnormal, which has strong systemic foundations. In the long term, these foundations may be more important to knowledge engineering than the techniques currently based on them. However, this chapter concentrates on the repertory grid as a technique for eliciting information from an expert.

3. WHAT IS A REPERTORY GRID?

A repertory grid is a two-way classification of data in which events are interlaced with abstractions in such a way as to express part of a person's system of cross-references between his *personal observations* or experience of the world (*elements*) and his *personal constructs* or classifications of that experience.

The *elements* are the things that are used to define the area of the topic, and they can be concrete or abstract entities. For example, in the context of interpersonal relations, the elements might be people; in attitudes to life, they might be critical events; in job change, they might be careers; in expertise about metal joining, they might be types of rivet; in expertise about medical diagnosis, they might be symptoms. Before choosing the set of elements, the user must think carefully about the area of the topic and relate the elements to his purpose. The elements should be of the same type and level of complexity, and should span the topic as fully as possible. It is usual to start with about 6 to 12 elements.

The universe of discourse is determined by the elements. The elements originally suggested by Kelly in his work as a psychotherapist were role titles such as Self, Mother, Father, Best Friend, Threatening Person, Rejected Teacher. This has been carried over into industry, with such role titles as Myself, My Boss, My Boss's Boss, Subordinate, Person Likely to Get On, Person Not Likely to Get On. The subject in both cases is required to supply names of individuals well known to her/him to fit these and other roles as closely as possible. When choosing elements care must be taken to ensure that each one is well known and personally meaningful to the subject. Each construct must be central to the person in the context of the particular problem.

The *constructs* are the terms in which the elements are similar to or different from each other. Each construct therefore has two *poles*, each of which has a meaning with respect to its opposite. Any construct or dimension of thinking that is important to the subject is a valid construct. For example, to distinguish between people by saying that x and y are "blue-eyed" whereas b and c are "brown-eyed" may be trivial and not concerned with the important qualities of x, y, b, and c. However, if you are an eye specialist concerned with prescribing tinted contact lenses, this may be a significant construct. Thoughts and feelings, objective and subjective descriptions, attitudes, and rules of thumb all constitute valid constructs. The verbal description of the construct and the labeling of the poles need not be a publically agreed meaning in the outside world, but only a memory aid to the thinking process. The mapping of the elements onto the constructs produces the two-dimensional grid of relationships.

3.1. ELICITING CONSTRUCTS

The most common method used for eliciting a construct is the minimal context form or triad method. The elements are presented in groups of three, three being the lowest number that will produce both a similarity and a difference, and the subject is asked to say in what way two are alike and thereby different from the third. This is the *emergent pole* of the construct. The *implicit pole* may be elicited by the difference method (in what way does the singleton differ from the pair) or by the opposite method (what would be the opposite of the description of the pair).

As an example, thinking of the three Artificial Intelligence books, *Handbook of AI*, *Winston's AI*, and *AI Applications for Business*, in what way are two alike and thereby different from the other one? We might first of all say that *Handbook of AI* and *AI Applications for Business* are alike since they are *multiauthored*, whereas *Winston's AI* is *single-authored*. This is, then, the first construct with its two poles or opposite descriptions. Now all the elements in the set must be rated on this dimension as either (1) being multiauthored or (2) being single-authored, as shown in Figure 1. This also shows the significance of the term *personal* in "personal con-

```
        1            1  2  3  4  5  6  7          2
                     ***********************

multiauthored  1  2  1  2  1  1  1   single-authored

                     ********************
                     *  *  *  *  *  *  Building Expert Systems
                     *  *  *  *  *  Logic Programming
                     *  *  *  *  Knowledge-Based Systems in AI
                     *  *  *  Winston & Horn LISP
                     *  *  AI Applications for Business
                     *  Winston's AI
                     Handbook of AI
```

FIGURE 1. A repertory grid with a single construct.

```
        1            1  2  3  4  5  6  7          2
                     *********************

multiauthored   1   2  1  2  1  1  1   single-authored

  theoretical   1   1  2  1  2  1  2   building systems

  fun to read   1   2  1  2  1  1  2   hard work

                     *********************
                     *   *   *   *   *   *   Building Expert Systems
                     *   *   *   *   *   Logic Programming
                     *   *   *   *   Knowledge-Based Systems in AI
                     *   *   *   Winston & Horn LISP
                     *   *   AI Applications for Business
                     *   Winston's AI
                     Handbook of AI
```

FIGURE 2. A repertory grid with three constructs.

struct" since it would not obviously be a publicly agreed description that
Winston and Horn's LISP is single-authored whereas the Davis and
Lenat book is multiauthored. In this case it reflects a single concerted
effort as opposed to more than one topic.

Then the second and subsequent constructs are elicited in exactly
the same way using different triads each time. Figure 2 shows the grid of
Figure 1 with a further two constructs elicited. The third construct
shown here illustrates that constructs can be factual, imaginary, emo-
tional, or whatever is important to the person generating the grid.

A scale allowing more distinctions than the pair 1 and 2 may be

```
        1            1  2  3  4  5  6  7          5
                     *********************

multiauthored   1   5  1  3  2  1  1   single-authored

  theoretical   1   1  4  2  4  1  5   building systems

  fun to read   2   3  2  5  1  1  5   hard work

                     *********************
                     *   *   *   *   *   *   Building Expert Systems
                     *   *   *   *   *   Logic Programming
                     *   *   *   *   Knowledge-Based Systems in AI
                     *   *   *   Winston & Horn LISP
                     *   *   AI Applications for Business
                     *   Winston's AI
                     Handbook of AI
```

FIGURE 3. A repertory grid with three constructs rated on a 5-point scale.

used as required. If a 1-to-5 scale is used, then the above example might become the grid shown in Figure 3. Thus, in this case, the third construct means that *Logic Programming* and *Knowledge-Based Systems in AI* are considered the most *fun to read* books, *Winston's AI* is both *fun to read* and *hard work*, and *Building Expert Systems* and *Winston and Horn LISP* are the most *hard work*.

Note how the use of a multipoint scale with an odd number of values allows for a central rating, in this case 3, which does not force the user to choose either pole. It may be desirable to apply more discrimination to this central rating and allow the subject the choice of the two possibilities: *neither*, that the element belongs to neither pole; or *both*, that the element belongs to both poles (Landfield, 1976). It is also possible to extend these possibilities to allow separate rating on each pole (Gaines and Shaw, 1981b; Shaw and Gaines, 1980).

4. TECHNIQUES FOR REPERTORY GRID ELICITATION AND ANALYSIS

In the past, the elicitation of repertory grids has been a task requiring a skilled psychologist who can draw out a person's constructs while not imposing his own ideas or personality. This has involved the development of a variety of techniques and methodologies for grid elicitation (Kelly, 1955; Fransella and Bannister, 1977). The coming of powerful, low-cost personal computers has made it possible to program some of the elicitation techniques used by people in a form where they can be applied automatically. It is now possible to codify some of the techniques used by people in a form where they can be administered through a conversational interactive computer program. PLANET contains two such programs: PEGASUS, which elicits a single grid from a person and feeds back comments and suggestions during the elicitation; and ARGUS, which elicits a set of grids from a person using a number of different perspectives.

An example of PEGASUS in action is given later in this paper. ARGUS elicits a set of grids simultaneously from one person holding several roles or points of view. First, the elements (roles) are elicited, followed by three constructs from fixed triads. These construct labels are then used for a new set of ratings to be entered for each role name in turn, and at each stage another construct that is felt to be important for that role is added. The final set of grids all with the same element and construct labels can be processed with the structure analysis programs SOCIOGRIDS, CORE, or MINUS, described below.

4.1. Repertory Grid Analysis

Repertory grids in themselves encode information about a person's way of looking at the world. This information can be used in its own right for some purposes since it is an aid to remembering the basis for decisions and actions. It can also be analyzed in a variety of ways to bring out possible underlying structures, or *construct systems*, in a person's world view and its relationship to those of others. There are a number of forms of analysis that are widely used for different purposes, and PLANET offers all the commonly used techniques plus new developments in recent years. What form of analysis should be used in a particular case is partly a matter of personal preference and partly a matter of purpose. Comparisons have been made in the literature of different analyses with the same data (Shaw, 1981), and if someone is using repertory grids for the first time, it is worth exploring the different techniques on their own data.

It is convenient to divide analysis techniques into three groups: those concerned with the analysis of a single grid, those concerned with a pair of grids, and those concerned with a group of grids.

4.2. Analysis of a Single Grid

For any given construct we may regard the numbers in the grid as a *vector of values* giving the assignment of each element in turn to one or another of the poles of the construct. From this point of view each construct becomes represented as a point in a multidimensional space whose dimension is the number of elements involved. A natural relation to examine between constructs is then the *distance* between them in this space. Two constructs that are zero distance apart are such that all elements are construed in the same way in relation to them, and hence we might infer that they are being used in the same way—in some sense they are *equivalent* constructs. For constructs that are not equivalent, we may analyze the entire constellation in space to determine a set of axes such that the projection of each construct onto the first axis accounts for most of the distance between them, the projection on the second axis accounts for most of the remaining distance, and so on. This is a *principal components analysis* of the construct space, and it is related to the *factor analysis* of semantic space used in the study of semantic differentials. We may also group constructs together that are close together in space using some form of *cluster analysis.*

The FOCUS algorithm is a distance-based hierarchical cluster analysis technique that sorts the constructs into a linear order such that constructs closest together in the space are also closest together in the order.

It has the advantage in presentation that the sorting is used only to represent the original grid reorganized by the "neighborness" of constructs and elements. It is left to the user to construe his own personal meaning into the result and confirm this directly in terms of the original data. Element and construct matching scores are computed by subtracting the rating values in each position of the two elements or constructs, summing them, then mapping the result into 0 to 100% similarity for the elements, and -100 to 100% similarity for the constructs. Two matrices are thus formed, one for elements and one for constructs. Clusters are computed by selecting the highest numbers from these matrices—that is, the most similar in terms of the ratings given—then continuing this process for the next cluster until all elements and constructs are incorporated. The tree diagrams show these clusters and are imposed on the resorted original grid data (Shaw, 1980).

The PRINGRID algorithm is another distance-based cluster analysis using standard principal component analysis techniques and giving the same results as Slater's INGRID (Slater, 1976, 1977). This analysis has been used widely in clinical studies with the repertory grid because it gives a visually meaningful "map" of some of the relations between elements and constructs. However, both INGRID and FOCUS are less applicable to knowledge engineering for expert systems where a logical analysis is more relevant.

The alternative to distance-based methods of grid analysis is a logical analysis, looking at constructs as predicates applying to elements. The ENTAIL algorithm derives asymmetric implications between the construct poles so that one can infer how a new element might be placed on one construct given how it is placed on others. This is discussed in more detail with the example given in a later section.

4.3. ANALYSIS OF A PAIR OF GRIDS

There are often times when it is desirable to compare several repertory grids. Shaw (1980) discusses *exchange grids* for the measurement of understanding and agreement between either two people or two occasions. To do this, two people, possibly experts with differing points of view, each elicit a grid in an area of common knowledge or experience. Each may choose his own elements independently of the other and may elicit and rate his constructs quite separately. Each then makes two copies of his grid, leaving out the rating values. Both these copies are filled in by the other person, one as he himself uses those constructs on those elements and the other as he thinks the original was completed. By comparing pairs of these grids it is possible to map the extent of overlap of the *agreement* and *understanding* between the two people.

There are three methods that can be used to compare two grids. The first is to concatenate the grids having the same elements and use the algorithms of FOCUS, ENTAIL, or PRINGRID as if they were one large grid. One can then explore the interaction of ideas by examining mixed clusters of constructs from the two grids.

A second way is to use the MINUS algorithm, which requires the two grids to have the same element and construct names, and highlights the differences between them by subtracting ratings in equivalent positions. The result shows where there was agreement indicated by areas of blanks, and grades of difference indicated by increasing numbers.

A third way is to use the CORE algorithm, again starting with two grids having the same element and construct names. CORE examines the most changed element and construct alternately, identifies it, and allows it to be deleted from the grids. In this way the core elements and constructs that show agreement or understanding in the two grids are identified and recorded.

4.4. ANALYSIS OF A GROUP OF GRIDS

The SOCIOGRIDS algorithm analyzes a set of repertory grids elicited from a group who share the same elements. It compares every pair of grids using the FOCUS algorithm and produces a set of *socionets*, which indicates the links of similar construing within the group. A *mode grid* is also produced showing the constructs that are readily understood by the majority of the group, and this is filed for future processing on one of the structure analysis programs. Every construct that has been used is listed in order of how highly matched it is across all grids, and indicating where it originated.

This technique can be used for a wide variety of purposes concerned with group structures, cultures, and relationships. It has been used for investigating the relative positions of members of a small group, and the content of the shared terms and values. It has been used to investigate management hierarchies defined operationally through the interrelationships of construct systems, and in conjunction with the Delphi technique to promote common values and understanding in a group.

5. SOFT SYSTEMS ANALYSIS

Personal construct psychology provides cognitive foundations for knowledge elicitation, and repertory grid techniques provide a corresponding methodology. However, neither in itself gives a framework for carrying out knowledge engineering. This section considers such a framework, Checkland's (1981) *soft systems analysis,* which is consistent with PCP and can be operationalized using repertory grid elicitation and analysis.

5.1. The Significance of Different Perspectives

Kelly emphasizes the *dynamic* and *personal* nature of the construct system. It is subject to change according to feedback from failure to anticipate events. It is individualistic in the constructs used, in the vocabulary used to name the construct poles, in the relations between constructs in the hierarchy, and in those constructs most likely to change when some change takes place.

Knowledge engineering for ESs may be seen as a process of making overt the construct system of the expert. The problems noted in the first section arise because of the essentially individualistic nature of construct systems. A person may be able to use his construction system effectively while having no basis for communicating it to others. Two people may use exactly the same construct yet refer to its poles by different names. Two people may use the same names for the poles of their constructs and yet use them in different ways. Two people may use similar constructs at the lower level of the hierarchy and yet have them organized in different systems such that their reactions to the same event are quite different. Two people may have similar constructs at nearly all levels of the hierarchy and yet construe a novel event completely differently.

This essentially *soft* aspect of the systems analysis of expert knowledge is contrary to the normal expectation that there is a "right" answer, valid for all conditions. Checkland (1981) has termed this a problem of soft systems analysis and emphasized the importance of the analyst's not bringing his own preconceptions to the problem domain. He has also shown the significance to taking into account a number of different perspectives in knowledge engineering.

5.2. Techniques of Soft Systems Analysis

Checkland (1981) has developed a number of techniques for soft systems analysis, starting with a structuring of the stages involved as shown in Figure 4.

The importance of Stage 1 is to get back to it from Stage 2 or beyond. We should not inject preconceptions about solutions into the problem definition and need to treat any situation as unstructured no matter

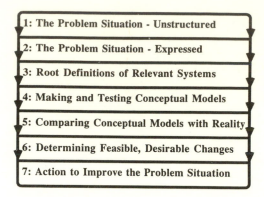

FIGURE 4. Stages in soft systems methodology.

what structure we are given. Our framework for analyzing the expert's knowledge may be such as to prevent that analysis. The expression at Stage 2 is still unstructured, and it is Checkland's study of Stage 3, *root definitions* of relevant systems, that provides the formal framework for a structure.

Checkland's approach is particularly interesting because it emphasizes the pluralism of systems analysis, what Kelly has termed *constructive alternativism*, that it is important to examine the problem from a number of viewpoints. These may be seen as forming a nested set to which Checkland gives the mnemonic CATWOE, as shown in Figure 5.

The system is defined through a Transformation carried out by people who are the Actors within it; it affects beneficially or adversely

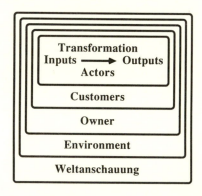

FIGURE 5. Root definitions of relevant systems.

other people who are its Customers, and there is some agency with power of existence over it who is its Owner; it has to exist within outside constraints forming its Environment, and the whole activity of system definition takes place within an ethos or *Weltanschauung* that affects our views of it. Basden (1983) has noted the utility of Checkland's analysis in developing ESs, and we have shown how the techniques outlined in this chapter may be applied to operationalizing it (Shaw and Gaines, 1983b).

Applying the analysis to an ES for oil exploration, we consider a *transformation* to which the *inputs* are survey data and the *outputs* are decisions to drill. The *actors* are experts concerned with making these decisions. Their *customers* are oil companies. The *owner* of the problem represents the value system, and, as usual in soft systems analysis, there are several choices: The managers, directors, and owners of the oil company are possibilities, as are its customers and the government that taxes it. They have differing perceptions of the problem, risk/reward ratios, and so on. The *environment* is the physical, geographic, and economic world within which extraction takes place, and the *Weltanshauung* comprises energy policies, pollution concerns, and so on. These are the considerations that knowledge engineering has to take into account.

The emphasis on differing viewpoints here is fundamental. PCP is often seen as concerned with the different perspectives of individuals, and knowledge engineering is often presented as concerned with the expert. However, particularly in complex real-life situations, it is rare to find all the expertise concentrated in one individual, and we are most often concerned with skills that reside in a group or team. In fact, the theory underlying PCP makes no separation necessary between the individual and the group (Shaw and Gaines, 1981a). We have shown elsewhere how it accounts for the way in which communities are formed by individuals and the way in which social norms in communities also act to form individuals (Shaw, 1985). The individual can be regarded as a cross section of the epistemological hierarchy of the community in which he is operating (Shaw, 1983). These considerations are those of Pask's *conversation theory* (Pask, 1975), particularly the notion of expertise distributed across a multiperson *P-Individual,* and it is notable that this theory is being used as a foundation for the development of ESs (Coombs and Alty, 1984).

Checkland's methodology structures the task of knowledge engineering and provides techniques that are widely applicable. However, it leaves the burden of analysis to a person and has no operational form as a computer program. The next sections show how the PCP approach can automate the analysis in major part.

6. PLANET: A COMPUTER-BASED KNOWLEDGE-ENGINEERING SYSTEM

The program system that we have developed for doing soft systems analysis from a variety of viewpoints and then comparing and contrasting the systems elicited is called PLANET (Personal Learning, Analysis, Negotiation, and Elicitation Techniques; Shaw, 1982). It runs as a menu-driven suite of interactive programs on a variety of computers, and, while preliminary versions were developed on the PDP10, there proved to be no difficulty in issuing PLANET for the Apple II, enabling its widespread use in field studies. The programs are all concerned with repertory grid elicitation and analysis, and they divide naturally into the following four groups.

Construct Elicitation. PEGASUS is a highly interactive program that elicits constructs through a conversational dialogue with an expert, generated by feedback of its ongoing analysis of his construct system. PEGASUS offers many options, one of which is to receive feedback from a stored bank of expert constructs, thus enabling a student to learn to use an expert's construct system. ARGUS is a variant of PEGASUS that puts one individual in the position of several others and elicits his view of their viewpoints as well as his own.

Single Construct System Analysis. FOCUS provides a hierarchical clustering of an expert's construct system that preserves the data elicited from him so that the sources of the analysis are evident and can be discussed. PRINGRID is a nonhierarchical cluster analysis based on principal components that can be used to gauge the major dimensions along which distinctions are being made. ENTAIL is a logical analysis of the construct system taking the expert's distinctions to be fuzzy predicates (Gaines, 1976; Zadeh, 1972). The entailment structure it generates can be used as a decision tree expressing the relationship between an expert's data and his conclusions. It can also provide rules for input to an ES shell (Boose, 1985; Gaines and Shaw, 1985).

Multiple Construct System Analysis. MINUS compares two grids based on the same elements and constructs to highlight the differences between them. CORE provides an interactive comparison of such grids to determine where there are differences and extract invariancies, e.g., over time. SOCIOGRIDS analyzes the total construct structure generated by a number of people construing the same elements from their individual viewpoints. It produces *socionets* showing the relationships be-

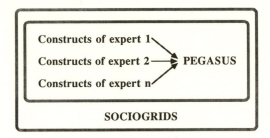

FIGURE 6. PLANET automating integration of multiple viewpoints.

tween individual construct systems within the group and a *mode grid* reflecting the constructs shared across the group.

Database Administration. DATA, INPUT, OUTPUT, and other programs within PLANET provide the facilities needed to manage the large databases of construct data generated from field studies of expertise.

PLANET provides a set of tools for the knowledge engineer enabling him to operate at Stage 3 of Checkland's soft systems analysis semi-automatically. As shown in Figure 6, PEGASUS enables the construct systems of all those involved in the application of expertise to be elicited. The experts involved can all be similar in nature or could have very different perspectives, such as "actor," "customer," and "owner". SOCIOGRIDS enables the consensual structure to be derived from the PEGASUS results, and ENTAIL enables this to be turned into a decision tree, or rules to prime an expert system shell, when appropriate.

The next section shows a sample of the PEGASUS dialogue in eliciting expertise from a manager in the appraisal of his subordinates (Shaw, 1980).

7. PEGASUS IN ACTION

PEGASUS commences its interaction by asking for the purpose of the elicitation and then for a set of elements relevant to this purpose, as shown in Figure 7. It is important to establish an initial context such that the expert selects a set of elements that are of the same type and relevant to the purpose of the elicitation. Note that in the dialogue the computer output is shown in normal face and the human input in italics.

One technique used by PEGASUS to elicit constructs is that of triadic comparison, as shown in Figure 8. A combination of three elements is

```
Type in your purpose for doing this grid?staff appraisal

Name six elements.

You must choose a set of six elements keeping in mind why you
want to do this grid. They could be people, events, pieces of
music, pictures, books, or what you want, but whatever you
choose they must be of the same type and each must be well
known to you. Try to choose specific things. Now type each
one after each question mark.

Do not forget to press the RETURN key after each.

     Element 1?S1
     Element 2?S2
     Element 3?S3
     Element 4?S4
     Element 5?S5
     Element 6?S6

Here is a list of your elements.

     1    S1
     2    S2
     3    S3
     4    S4
     5    S5
     6    S6

Do you want to change an element?no

Can you think of another element that belongs with the 6 that
you have got so far?y

     Element 7?S7
```

FIGURE 7. PEGASUS initial element selection.

the minimum necessary to establish both a similarity and a difference. The poles of personal constructs are not just a logical predicate and its negation. Construing the three elements sets up a context, or a perspective, which corresponds to the logical notion of *relevance*. The two poles of the construct anchor the extremal ends of the dimension of construing that defines this relevance.

Another technique used by PEGASUS to elicit constructs is that of matching the ratings given to elements and asking for a construct that differentiates between two highly matched elements, as shown in Figure 9.

A technique that allows PEGASUS to elicit additional elements is to match constructs across elements and ask for a new element that differentiates between two highly matched constructs, as shown in Figure 10.

Through a combination of triadic comparison, element matching, and construct matching, as shown in the flow chart of Figure 11, a PEGASUS interaction elicits from the user his system of constructs relating to the topic being studied. Figure 12 is the final grid of the manager.

```
Triad for elicitation of construct 1
  1 S1
  2 S2
  3 S3

Can you choose two of this triad of elements which are in
some way alike and different from the other one?

What is the number of the one which is different?3

Now I want you to think about what you have in mind when you
separate the pair from the other one. How can you describe
the two ends or poles of the scale which discriminate S1 and
S2 on the left pole from S3 on the right pole?

Just type one or two words for each pole to remind you what
you are thinking or feeling when you use this construct.

    left pole rated 1 --?intelligent
    right pole rated 5 --?dim

Now assume that S1 and S2 are assigned the value 1 and S3 is
assigned the value 5. According to how you feel about them,
please assign to each of the other elements in turn a
provisional value from 1 to 5.

  1 S1    1
  2 S2    1
  3 S3    5
  4 S4    ?5
  5 S5    ?3
  6 S6    ?3
  7 S7    ?5
  8 S8    ?2
  9 S9    ?3
```

FIGURE 8. PEGASUS triadic construct elicitation.

```
The two elements 5 S5 and 6 S6 are matched at the 90 percent
level. This means that so far you have not distinguished
between S5 and S6.

Do you want to split these?y

Think of a construct which separates these two elements, with
S5 on the left pole and S6 on the right pole.

    left pole rated 1 --?self starters
    right pole rated 5 --?need a push

According to how you feel about them, please assign to each of
the other elements in turn a provisional value from 1 to 5.

  5 S5     1
  6 S6     5
  1 S1    ?2
  2 S2    ?1
  3 S3    ?5
  4 S4    ?5
  7 S7    ?5
  8 S8    ?3
  9 S9    ?4
 10 S10   ?5
```

FIGURE 9. PEGASUS construct elicitation by breaking element match.

```
The two constructs you called
   1 intelligent -- dim
   4 little supervision reqd -- need supervision
are matched at the 66 percent level

This means that most of the time you are saying intelligent
you are also saying little supervision reqd and most of the
time you are saying dim you are also saying need supervision.
Think of another element which is either intelligent and need
supervision or little supervision reqd and dim. If you really
cannot do this, then just press RETURN after the first
question mark, but please try.

Then you must give this element a rating value on each
construct in turn. After each question mark type a value from
1 to 5.

What is your element?S10

Type in the ratings for this element on each construct.
Left pole rated 1, right pole rated 5.

   intelligent -- dim?5
   willing -- unwilling?2
   new boy -- old sweats?3
   little supervision reqd -- need supervision?3
```

FIGURE 10. PEGASUS element elicitation by breaking construct match.

8. ENTAIL IN ACTION

ENTAIL (Gaines and Shaw, 1981b, 1985; Shaw and Gaines, 1982) gives a dependency analysis of the grid by listing logical entailments consistent with the data. The dependency analysis is also being extended to be interactive so that it may lead to the elicitation of further elements if the system suggests dependencies with which the expert disagrees, or to the modification of ratings if the expert suggests dependencies that are not possible according to the data he has entered. The overall objective is to allow the expert to explore the dimensions of his conceptual structure, testing it against specific cases, and discussing its implications, until he is comfortable that the representation elicited reasonably represents his knowledge.

Figure 13 shows the ENTAIL analysis of the grid of Figure 12. The entailments are shown with three values, the first a truth value from 0 to 100 (e.g., L 9 → L 13 truth 100), the second the probability of the hypothesis being true, and the third the uncertainty reduction generated by asserting this entailment. All three are in the range from 0 to 100. The uncertainty reduction measures the information carried by the assertion and is used to ensure that trivial entailments consistent with the data are pruned (Gaines and Shaw, 1985).

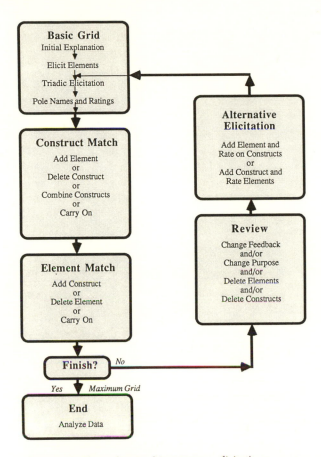

FIGURE 11. Flow of control in PEGASUS elicitation.

In our initial analysis of entailment we introduced the notion of entailments being true "usually" and interpreted this as "in all except one instance." The original version of ENTAIL generates entailments that are usually true, and these have proved useful with some data where there is a common pattern upset only by an isolated case. The concept of "usually" can be generalized and formalized within the framework already established, and it leads to an interesting two-dimensional analysis of fuzzy data.

We quantify the notion of a hypothesis being true "usually" by ascribing a probability to the hypothesis measured by the relative frequency with which it is true. For example, using the data of L9 and L13, L9 → L13 has truth value 1 with probability 1; it is always absolutely

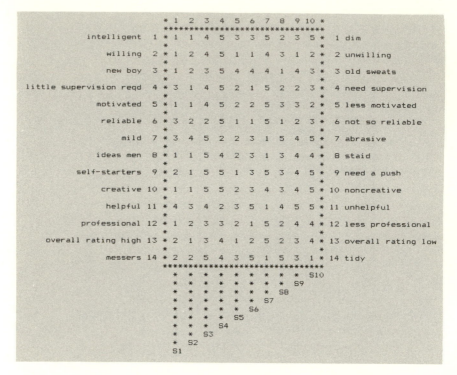

FIGURE 12. PEGASUS repertory grid elicited on staff appraisal.

true. However, L13 → L9 is more interesting because it has truth value 0.5 with probability 1, truth value 0.75 with probability 0.9 (fails in 1 case out of 10), and truth value 1.0 with probability 0.4 (fails in 6 cases out of 10).

This type of trade-off distribution between the truth value of an assertion and its probability of being true occurs in inductive inference with fuzzy data, for example, in inferring structure from fuzzy sequential data (Gaines, 1979). We can evaluate the possible trade-offs by using the uncertainty reduction analysis based on expected surprise already described by Gaines and Shaw (1985b).

ENTAIL checks for equivalence separately from the check for one-way entailment. This is because the uncertainty reduction from the hypothesis of equivalence, $x \equiv y$, cannot be inferred from the separate uncertainty reductions of the logically equivalent pair of hypotheses, $x \rightarrow y$ and $y \rightarrow x$, although it will be at least the sum of these. In order to rank-order the hypotheses, the uncertainty reduction for one-sided entailment is doubled for comparison with that of two-sided equivalence.

Note how a hypothesis of high truth value, such as R13 → R9, can give less information reduction than one of lower truth value, such as L1 → L9. Note also how a one-sided hypothesis, such as L1 → L10, may give greater uncertainty reduction than its two-sided equivalent, L1 ≡ L10, and hence have a higher ranking. Similarly, the two one-sided hypotheses, such as L9 → L10 and L10 → L9, can also occur in preference to the two-sided hypotheses, L9 ≡ L10. The list of hypotheses in Figure 13 has been terminated when the uncertainty reduction falls below 35% for a two-sided hypothesis. It can be truncated at any level and the entailments plotted in graphical form. However, since approximate inference is involved, the graph will not necessarily be transitive, and it

```
Entail    Truth Prob.  Information (Cutoff 35)

L  9 → L13   100   100   59  self-starters → overall rating high
L  1 → L  9    75   100   58  intelligent → self-starters
L10 → L  8   100   100   57  creative → ideas men
R  9 → R  1    75   100   56  need a push → dim
L  1 → L10    75   100   52  intelligent → creative
R  8 → R10   100   100   52  staid → noncreative
R13 → R  6    75   100   52  overall rating low → not so reliable
L10 → L  9    75   100   51  creative → self-starters
R10 → R  1    75   100   49  noncreative → dim
L  9 → L10    75   100   47  self starters → creative
L10 ≡ L  1    75   100   47  creative ≡ intelligent
R  1 ≡ R10    75   100   47  dim ≡ noncreative
R  9 ≡ R10    75   100   47  need a push ≡ noncreative
R13 → R  9   100   100   46  overall rating low → need a push
R  4 → R13    75   100   44  need supervision → overall rating low
R  5 → R  4    75   100   44  less motivated → need supervision
R  5 → R13    75   100   44  less motivated → overall rating low
L  1 → L  3    75   100   42  intelligent → new boy
L  6 → L13    75   100   42  reliable → overall rating high
L  4 ≡ L13    75   100   39  little supervision reqd ≡ overall rating high
L13 ≡ L  6    75   100   39  overall rating high ≡ reliable
R  1 → R  6    50   100   39  dim → not so reliable
R  6 ≡ R13    75   100   39  not so reliable ≡ overall rating low
R13 ≡ R  4    75   100   39  overall rating low ≡ need supervision
R12 → R13    75   100   38  less professional → overall rating low
R13 → R12    75   100   38  overall rating low → less professional
L  8 ≡ L10   100    70   37  ideas men ≡ creative
R  9 → R  4    50   100   37  need a push → need supervision
R  9 → R12    50   100   37  need a push → less professional
R  9 → R13    50   100   37  need a push → overall rating low
R10 ≡ R  8   100    70   37  noncreative ≡ staid
L  4 → L  5    75   100   36  little supervision reqd → motivated
L  4 → L  9    50   100   36  little supervision reqd → self-starters
L12 → L  9    50   100   36  professional → self-starters
L12 ≡ L13    75   100   36  professional ≡ overall rating high
L13 → L  5    75   100   36  overall rating high → motivated
L13 → L  9    50   100   36  overall rating high → self-starters
R  2 → R  4    75   100   35  unwilling → need supervision
R  2 → R  5    75   100   35  unwilling → less motivated
R  2 → R13    75   100   35  unwilling → overall rating low
R  3 → R  1    75   100   35  old sweats → dim
```

FIGURE 13. Entailment analysis of repertory grid on staff appraisal.

is important to preserve the intransitivity. It avoids the paradoxes of approximate reasoning, such as that of iterated approximate inference— for example, that a person with one more hair than a bald man is still bald (Gaines, 1976, 1983).

The entailments derived by ENTAIL can be converted directly to rules that may be loaded into a standard ES shell, as Boose (1985) has shown. The truth value of the rule codes into the truth value representation used by the shell. The rules may be checked by the expert for their content, but their prior evaluation for uncertainty reduction makes it unlikely that spurious rules will be generated. The rules form a decision tree expressing the relationship between an expert's data and his conclusions, both personally expressed. For example, the data of Figure 12 may be regarded as those of an expert on staff appraisal concerned with deriving his "overall rating" (construct 13) from behavioral assessments such as "intelligent" and "creative." The ENTAIL analysis of Figure 13 shows that L1, L4, L6, L9, L10, and L12 imply L13, that "intelligent, creative, reliable, and professional self-starters requiring little supervision receive a high overall rating," whereas R2, R4, R5, R6, R9, and R12 imply R13, that "being unwilling, less motivated, not so reliable, less professional, needing supervision, and needing a push leads to a low overall rating."

9. VALIDATION

The methodology described is very easy to implement and run. Experts enjoy using the system and need far less attention from a knowledge engineer. It is important initially that the expert gain some familiarity with the construing and rating process. It is essential that the expert become familiar with the kinds of questions being asked, and finish his grid with a representative set of elements all at the same level of abstraction, and a representative set of constructs that cover all cases. The best way to achieve this is not through discussion but by experience in the informal use of PLANET, construing books, movies, friends as an exercise before undertaking the main knowledge elicitation.

We put great emphasis on the need to be able to *validate* any technique for knowledge engineering. It is not sufficient to show that reasonable expert systems can be developed. One must attempt to evaluate the accuracy and completeness of the knowledge transfer. This is not an easy task because there are few well-established domains of expertise where the accuracy of the elicitation can be tested. One needs clear-cut test cases where the conceptual framework of experts has been both elicited and validated. Sowa (1984) describes one such case where the record-keeping needs of a business can be prescribed through the BIAIT analysis technique (Carlson, 1979), based on seven features, such as "Does the supplier bill the customer, or does the customer pay cash?" and "Does the supplier deliver the product at some time in the future, or does the customer take the order with him?"

A study has been carried out using PLANET to determine whether PEGASUS can be used to elicit the BIAIT distinctions from those with some accounting or business knowledge (Shaw, 1984). The experiments have been based on taking a spectrum of those with assumed expertise in business record keeping, from businessmen and accountants to accounting students at various stages of their education, and using PEGASUS to elicit their constructs relating to business transactions. Again, in the interests of an initial open-ended approach, the construing has not been tightly constrained to relate to the record-keeping aspects of the transactions. It has been interesting to determine what distinctions are made that do not relate to record keeping, or relate to it in ways different from BIAIT.

Various forms of analysis have been applied to the resulting grids. The constructs elicited have been compared with the BIAIT constructs by analyzing with ENTAIL the compound grids obtained by merging the constructs elicited from each person with those corresponding to the BIAIT constructs. This has shown that all the BIAIT constructs exist within those elicited. The set of grids obtained has also been analyzed with SOCIOGRIDS to see whether the variations of expertise across the group of subjects used shows up clearly. This is a good test of the basic validity of the technique and its foundations in the notion of construing. For example, in an earlier study (Shaw, 1980) of quality control for a garment company, the SOCIOGRIDS analysis reconstructed the management hierarchy of the firm from the construct systems of staff involved in construing garment faults.

The operation of SOCIOGRIDS is based on what Kelly terms the *commonality corollary* (Kelly, 1955) that to the extent that one person employs a construction of experience that subsumes that of another in a given domain, that person can understand the cognitive processes of the other person in that domain. Thus, an expert system for a domain can be defined as one that subsumes the relevant constructions of experience of experts in that domain. Figure 14 shows a socionet produced by SOCIO-GRIDS in which an arrow from one person to another shows that the first person "outconstrues" the other. The results are mainly what one

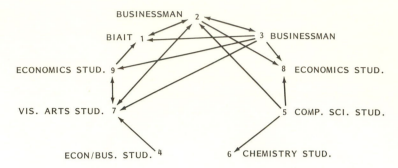

FIGURE 14. Socionet produced by SOCIOGRIDS from BIAIT validation experiment.

would expect, with the businessmen and the economics students closely related to BIAIT. The only disconcerting result is the position of the Visual Arts student, who is clearly a central part of the cluster. Enquiry into the background of this student revealed that she had only recently become a student, having spent the previous 25 years as an administrative secretary in an insurance organization.

The capability of PLANET and related systems to generate useful expert systems rapidly is clearly another important dimension of validation. Boose (1985) discusses the strengths and weaknesses of his Expertise Transfer System (ETS), which is based on the PLANET system but operates on a Xerox 1108 LISP machine. At Boeing Computer Services he has produced a wide range of expert systems by this methodology. He says that it is better suited for analysis than for synthesis problems—for example, debugging, diagnosis, interpretation, and classification rather than design and planning; that it is difficult to apply to "deep" causal knowledge or strategic knowledge. On the other hand he says: "Knowledge engineers feel that ETS can save at least two months of project calendar time. This estimate is made by comparing the time taken for knowledge acquisition for similar projects. The reduction in time results in savings of both the expert's time and the knowledge engineer's time" (Boose, 1985).

Figure 15 shows the screen of the LISP machine running (ETS) at the stage of generating conclusion rules from the grid ratings. ETS has been used to supply the initial knowledge base to TEIRESIAS (Davis and Lenat, 1982), which helps the expert and knowledge engineer to debug and refine an existing knowledge base since TEIRESIAS is not capable of eliciting such information on its own.

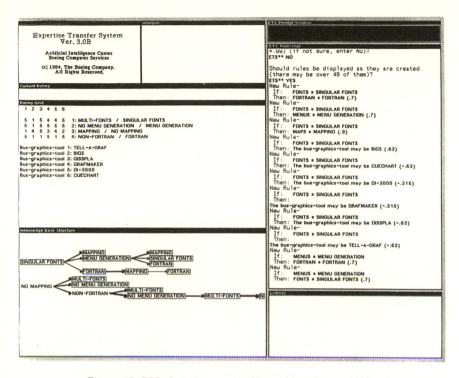

FIGURE 15. ETS elicitation on a LISP machine (Boose, 1985).

10. GUIDELINES SUMMARY

1. Kelly's personal construct psychology identifies the system of construction being used by an expert as fundamental to his thought processes.

2. Checkland's soft system analysis structures the application of these concepts to the ill-defined problems typical of expert system applications.

3. These methodologies can be used to structure interviews eliciting knowledge from experts.

4. However, manual elicitation is tedious, and on-line analysis and feedback lead to improved elicitation.

5. Automatic computer-based techniques have been developed and prove very effective in knowledge elicitation for expert systems.

6. PEGASUS is a program that elicits from an expert the fundamental distinctions, or constructs, he is using in applying his expertise.

7. ENTAIL analyzes the logical dependencies between constructs and can be used to develop rules for an ES shell.

8. SOCIOGRIDS analyzes the relations between experts and can be used to develop consensual construct systems.

9. The programs and methodology have been widely used since 1978 not only for expert system development but also for a wide variety of knowledge-elicitation studies in psychology, education, and management.

10. Studies have been carried out to validate the methodology experimentally using the BIAIT business record-keeping constructs as a standard.

11. Boeing Computer Services has implemented a related system, ETS, on a LISP machine and produced a wide range of expert systems in an industrial environment.

12. The methodology is better suited for analysis than for synthesis problems—for example, debugging, diagnosis, interpretation, and classification rather than design and planning.

13. It is currently difficult to apply to "deep" causal knowledge or strategic knowledge.

14. In situations where it is applicable, the methodology can save at least 2 months of project calendar time, and decision support systems can be prototyped in a few hours.

ACKNOWLEDGMENTS. Financial assistance for this work has been made available by the National Sciences and Engineering Research Council of Canada. We are grateful to Dr. John Boose and Boeing Computer Services for permission to use Figure 15.

11. REFERENCES

Bainbridge, L. (1979). Verbal reports as evidence of the process operator's knowledge. *International Journal of Man-Machine Studies, 11*(4), 411–436.

Basden, A. (1983). On the application of expert systems. *International Journal of Man-Machine Studies, 19*(5), 461–477.

Boose, J. H. (1985). A knowledge acquisition program for expert systems based on personal construct psychology. *International Journal of Man-Machine Studies, 23*(5), 495–525.

Carlson, W. M. (1979). The new horizon in business information analysis. *Data Base, 10*(4), 3–9.

Checkland, P. (1981). *Systems thinking, systems practice.* Chichester, England: Wiley.

Coombs, M., and Alty, J. (1984). Expert systems: An alternative paradigm. *International Journal of Man-Machine Studies, 20*(1), 21–43.

Davis, R., and Lenat, D. B. (1982). *Knowledge-based systems in artificial intelligence.* New York: McGraw-Hill.

Feigenbaum, E. A. (1980). *Knowledge engineering: The applied side of artificial intelligence.* Report STAN-CS-80-812. Department of Computer Science, Stanford University.

Fransella, F., and Bannister, D. (1977). *A manual for repertory grid technique.* London: Academic Press.

Freud, S. (1914). *Psychopathology of everyday life.* London: Benn.

Gaines, B. R. (1976). Foundations of fuzzy reasoning. *International Journal of Man-Machine Studies, 8*(6), 623–668.

Gaines, B. R. (1979). Sequential fuzzy system identification. *Fuzzy Sets and Systems, 2*(1), 15–24.

Gaines, B. R. (1983). Precise past—Fuzzy future. *International Journal of Man-Machine Studies, 19*(1), 117–134.

Gaines, B. R. (1984). Perspectives on fifth generation computing. *Oxford Surveys in Information Technology, 1*, 1–53.

Gaines, B. R., and Shaw, M. L. G. (1981a). A programme for the development of a systems methodology of knowledge and action. In W. J. Reckmeyer (Ed.), *General systems research and design: Precursors and futures.* (pp. 255–264). Louisville, Ky.: Society for General Systems Research.

Gaines, B. R., and Shaw, M. L. G. (1981b). New directions in the analysis and interactive elicitation of personal construct systems. In M. L. G. Shaw (Ed.), *Recent advances in personal construct technology* (pp. 147–182). London: Academic Press.

Gaines, B. R., and Shaw, M. L. G. (1986). Induction of inference rules for expert systems. *Fuzzy Sets and Systems, 18*, 315–328.

Gevarter, W. B. (1983). Expert systems: Limited but powerful. *IEEE Spectrum, 18*, 39–45.

Hawkins, D. (1983). An analysis of expert thinking. *International Journal of Man-Machine Studies, 18*(1), 1–47.

Hayes-Roth, F., Waterman, D. A., and Lenat, D. B. (Eds.). (1983). *Building expert systems.* Reading, Mass.: Addison-Wesley.

Kelly, G. A. (1955). *The psychology of personal constructs.* New York: Norton.

Landfield, A. (1976). A personal construct approach to suicidal behaviour. In P. Slater (Ed.), *Dimensions of intrapersonal space* (Vol. 1, pp. 93–107). London: Wiley.

Mancuso, J. R., and Adams-Webber, J. R. (Eds.). (1982). *The construing person.* New York: Praeger.

Michie, D. (Ed.). (1979). *Expert systems in the micro electronic age.* Edinburgh: Edinburgh University Press.

Moto-oka, T. (Ed.). (1982). *Fifth generation computer systems.* Amsterdam: North-Holland.

Pask, G. (1975). *Conversation, cognition and learning.* Amsterdam: Elsevier.

Pope. M. L., and Shaw, M. L. G. (1981). Personal construct psychology in education and learning. In M. L. G. Shaw (Ed.), *Recent advances in personal construct technology* (pp. 105–114). London: Academic Press.

Reitman, W. (Ed.). (1984). *Artificial intelligence applications for business.* Norwood, N.J.: Ablex.

Rogers, C. R. (1967). *On becoming a person: A therapist's view of psychotherapy.* London: Constable.

Shaw, M. L. G. (1980). *On becoming a personal scientist*. London: Academic Press.
Shaw, M. L. G. (Ed.). (1981). *Recent advances in personal construct technology*. London: Academic Press.
Shaw, M. L. G. (1982). PLANET: Some experience in creating an integrated system for repertory grid applications on a microcomputer. *International Journal of Man-Machine Studies, 17*(3), 345–360.
Shaw, M. L. G. (1983). Epistemological hierarchies in knowledge and expert systems. In J. P. van Gigch (Ed.), *Metamodels and metasystems*. Cambridge, Mass.: Abacus Press.
Shaw, M. L. G. (1984, May). Interactive knowledge elicitation. *Proceedings of CIPS SESSION 84* (pp. 202–208). Calgary: Canadian Information Processing Society.
Shaw, M. L. G. (1985). Communities of knowledge. In F. Epting and A. W. Landfield (Eds.), *Anticipating personal construct psychology* (pp. 25–35). Lincoln: University of Nebraska Press.
Shaw, M. L. G., and Gaines, B. R. (1980). Fuzzy semantics for personal construing. *Systems science and science* (pp. 146–154). Louisville, Ky.: Society for General Systems Research.
Shaw, M. L. G., and Gaines, B. R. (1981a). The personal scientist in the community of science. In W. J. Reckmeyer (Ed.), *General systems Research and design: Precursors and futures* (pp. 59–68). Louisville, Ky.: Society for General Systems Research.
Shaw, M. L. G., and Gaines, B. R. (1981b). The personal computer and the personal scientist. *BCS '81: Information technology for the eighties* (pp. 235–252). London: Heyden Press for British Computer Society.
Shaw, M. L. G., and Gaines, B. R. (1981c). Exploring personal semantic space. In B. Rieger (Ed.), *Empirical semantics II* (pp. 712–791). Bochum, West Germany: Studienverlag Brockmeyer.
Shaw, M. L. G., and Gaines, B. R. (1982). Eliciting entailment. In R. Trappl, L. Ricciardi, and G. Pask (Eds.), *Progress in cybernetics and systems research* (Vol. 9, pp. 425–435). Washington, D.C.: Hemisphere.
Shaw, M. L. G., and Gaines, B. R. (1983a, December). A computer aid to knowledge engineering. *Proceedings of British Computer Society conference on expert systems*, Cambridge, pp. 263–271.
Shaw, M. L. G., and Gaines, B. R. (1983b). Eliciting the real problem. In H. Wedde (Ed.), *International working conference on model realism* (pp. 100–111). Oxford: Pergamon Press.
Shaw, M. L. G., and Gaines, B. R. (1984). Deriving the constructs underlying decision. In H.-J. Zimmerman, B. R. Gaines, and L. A. Zadeh (Eds.), *Fuzzy sets and decision analysis. TIMS series studies in the management sciences*. Amsterdam: North-Holland.
Shaw, M. L. G., and Gaines, B. R. (1985). Some perspectives on knowledge engineering for expert systems and simulation. In *Proceedings of workshop on coupling symbolic and numerical computing in expert systems*. Bellevue, Wash.: Boeing Computer Services.
Shepherd, E., and Watson, J. P. (Eds.). (1982). *Personal meanings*. London: Wiley.
Slater, P. (Ed.). (1976). *Dimensions of intrapersonal space* (Vol. 1). London: Wiley.
Slater, P. (Ed.). (1977). *Dimensions of intrapersonal space* (Vol. 2). London: Wiley.
Sowa, J. F. (1984). *Conceptual structures: Information processing in mind and machine*. Reading, Mass.: Addison-Wesley.
Welbank, M. (1983). *A review of knowledge acquisition techniques for expert systems*. BTRL, Ipswich: Martlesham Consultancy Services.
Zadeh, L. A. (1972). Fuzzy languages and their relation to human intelligence. *Proceedings of the international conference on man and computer*. Basel: Karger.

7

Different Techniques and Different Aspects on Declarative Knowledge

JOHN G. GAMMACK

1. INTRODUCTION

In this chapter we describe techniques for discovering organization in an expert's domain knowledge. These techniques are illustrated in the domain of "domestic gas-fired hot water and central heating systems," which possesses technical properties seen as relevant to larger-scale domains. The informant was not a recognized expert on central heating but a scientist with an interest in the domain.

In an earlier paper (Gammack and Young, 1985), we noted that many expert systems force expert knowledge into a rule format whether such a format is appropriate or not, and it might be more useful to recognize that there are other conceivable aspects to an expert's knowledge. We identified some different forms of knowledge that seemed relevant for knowledge elicitation purposes, such as concepts, facts, procedures, and metaknowledge, and suggested that different elicitation techniques were applicable to these different kinds. Our chosen aspect of expert knowledge is the expert's conception of the domain, in which are represented terms of reference and their usual intended meaning, relationships perceived among these domain concepts, and organizational structure giving them a coherence for the expert. By the

JOHN G. GAMMACK • MRC Applied Psychology Unit, Cambridge CB2 2EF, England.

artifice of decoupling declarative domain "facts" from rules composing them, and from any perceived contextual knowledge to constrain the application of such rules, we take a more "modular" approach to elicitation, in which we first agree a set of domain facts, which of themselves imply nothing about how to use those facts.

Rather than being targeted at a particular application, our research aims to present techniques for declarative knowledge elicitation in general, and to indicate where they might be useful in our scheme. In the present chapter our concern is with elicitation of the structure of conceptual information upon which much knowledge-based behavior depends. This includes information on which concepts apply in a domain, what they mean, and what their relative place is in the domain, as seen by the expert. Other information relating the concepts to each other is elicited, as are differentiating criteria to distinguish them from similar concepts. This information is relevant when constructing a knowledge base that may be used with an expert system, since so much time is now spent by knowledge engineers trying to impose their own structure on the knowledge they are given. Information about the structure of a domain can help to organize further systematic elicitation using structured interview techniques.

Throughout this chapter we use the word *concepts* to designate the terms an expert uses to express domain knowledge. In the terminology of other fields, *concepts* might correspond to *objects* or *entities*; however, since these have specific meanings in fields from linguistics to data processing, we stay with *concepts* and hope that avoiding commitment to the terminology of a particular field will allow the ideas presented here to have more general application.

In practice, our concepts tend to be identified with nouns or compound nouns, such as *boiler, flow,* and *radiator control valve* in the present domain. Although concepts are clearly not just words, for practical purposes we define *concepts* to include idiosyncratic labels for ideas which the expert has but which may not be in public use. These are permitted so long as such concepts can have an agreed or public definition. The motivation for this is to allow representation of the richer set of concepts with which the expert actually *"thinks,"* as well as the language used for communication.

2. METHODS

The approach described here takes four consecutive phases, which are (1) eliciting component terms to be used for construction (concept elicitation), (2) eliciting some structure for those terms (structure elicitation), (3) formally representing that structure (structure representation), and then (4) transforming that representation to be used for some desired purpose.

Following Grover's (1983) suggestion that a pragmatic knowledge-acquisition methodology should have a glossary component, an agreed vocabulary is developed (the "Concept Elicitation" section, 2.1). This is done using a *tutorial interview*, from which is taken a vocabulary of concepts, which is then expertly defined.

Having this domain vocabulary then becomes the basis for a structuring of the concepts in the domain (the "Structure Elicitation" section, 2.2). This is done using a *card-sorting* technique and is supplemented with a *multidimensional scaling* task. It is assumed that part of expertise consists in being able to impose a useful organization on the basic concepts in order to manage it more effectively. Another chosen aspect of expert knowledge is the ability to make distinctions among similar concepts. This might be useful when considering differential diagnoses in a medical domain, or choosing among candidate statistical tests, for instance. Conversely, knowing which properties concepts have in common allows analogies to be drawn for a variety of purposes, and may be useful, for instance, when looking for an equivalent component for making temporary repairs. We suggest that the *repertory grid* technique is useful for eliciting such information.

In the "Structure Representation" section (2.3), we describe *proximity ratings* and the PATHFINDER analysis technique for representing the expert's conceptual organization. This is used to guide elicitation of propositional ("factual") information using a *matrix elicitation technique*, and this information is coded into a database. Many of the techniques described below are familiar from traditional psychology. The matrix elicitation technique is novel, but it has obvious affinities with standard systems methodology.

Following all this is a section showing one way in which this representation may be used; it is intended to be as much illustrative as prescriptive. In this section we use primitive procedures to examine the database thus created, and find what is in it.

2.1. CONCEPT ELICITATION

The first stage of concept elicitation was to ask the expert to prepare an introductory talk outlining the whole domain, then to deliver it as a tutorial session to the knowledge engineer. This format suited the particular expert, but since its main purpose was to generate concepts, the exact procedure is not critical. For this reason, too, any structure the expert might impose for didactic purposes, though of incidental interest, may not be considered important since it provides only one view of the knowledge. However, if the knowledge base is to be used for tutoring or training, such organizational information may well become relevant.

Other equivalent techniques possible at this stage include tape-recording a lecture, a structured or unstructured interview, or a protocol generated from talking through case histories, for instance. Less naturalistic experimental techniques also exist; for example, one direct method is simply to ask the expert to generate a list of typical concepts and then systematically to probe for more related information (e.g., using free association). Such methods await empirical work in the field of knowledge elicitation and might usefully be considered as variants of the interview technique. The important thing is that the chosen technique gets the expert communicating fluently, and it does not particularly matter about the overall organization. In well-understood domains, lists of concepts might already exist, for example, as an index to a manual. This could prove an adequate alternative.

In this case, preparation took about a quarter of an hour, and the talk itself lasted about 1 hour. The expert indicated throughout places where more detail could be given, if it was thought relevant. The informant's intuitions about how much to say about any particular thing seem important; clearly there are no hard-and-fast rules about what constitutes domain knowledge and what is more general detail. This also showed up weaker areas of the expert's knowledge.

The session was tape-recorded and the protocol was later transcribed. Labeled diagrams were also produced during the session. These helped the expert to construct the talk, and to clarify the protocol later to the knowledge engineer. One thing to be aware of if the protocol is to be used as a source of, say, knowledge about sequences of causality is that working from diagrams may be problematic if the expert points and uses anaphoric references (e.g., "and then *this* goes to *here* . . . "). Video promises to capture some aspects of such information but seems too expensive and impractical to be recommended. Instead, the knowledge engineer should look out for ambiguous pronouns and the like, and explicitly note these at the time, either on tape or on a pad.

In identifying possible contingencies, diagrams and other alternatives to prose (such as decision trees) are a neglected form of representation through which knowledge can be communicated. These may, however, be more convenient than natural language for certain types of knowledge communication (Wright, 1971, 1974).

Having the protocol transcribed is not strictly necessary for eliciting a list of concepts, but it allows opportunists to use the protocol as a source of other aspects of knowledge, such as heuristic rules and personal memories, if the relevant information in these can be represented.

From this transcript a number of concepts was extracted: In this case it was a trivial exercise to pick out about 90 nouns or compound nouns, both concrete and abstract in nature. In other domains, however, underlying abstract concepts may need to be inferred. The expert edited this list by removing synonyms, slips of the tongue, and other aberrant terms, which reduced the list to 75 familiar concepts. These are shown at the bottom level of Figure 1. The expert initially considered the dictionary definition of these concepts to be adequate, but since there is no guarantee that the expert's own definition necessarily matches the dictionary one, a personal definition of the concepts was later given. This took 1 hour and produced only a few new concepts, such as "fluid", "safety" and "room." These new concepts obviously do not entirely close the set of possibilities, but they appeared to be either generic forms of existing ideas or wider-context specific terms in nature. This seemed to suggest that most of the central domain concepts had already been captured. The definitions indicated that sometimes a concept went beyond the level of detail given in a general-purpose dictionary and sometimes it meant one very specific idea in the context of the domain.

This illustrates an important issue: Much human expertise is likely to consist in the personal and semantic associations (connotative meaning) that an expert brings to domain concepts and may result in the invention or appropriation of personalized terms to describe esoteric or subtle domain phenomena. Thus, while a dictionary (explicit) definition may well serve as a convenient consensus of referential meaning, it may fail to capture the full sense of the words used. This problem may be reduced by assuming that a concept gains fuller sense in regard to surrounding associates, but such a rounding out may be of more theoretical than practical value.

The domain glossary we obtained happened to be restricted substantially to the component parts of a central heating system, such as thermostats and radiators, but also included general physical terms such as *heat* and *gravity*. A second pass through the transcript yielded 42 relational concepts, usually verbs. Examples of these included "contains," "heats," "connects to." A similar glossary could be compiled for these concepts in an attempt to constrain the describable relations among the physical components to a well-specified set of possibilities. The motivation for partitioning the domain vocabulary this way is to facilitate a propositional representation, compatible with symbolic programming languages. This will be described later. The psychological

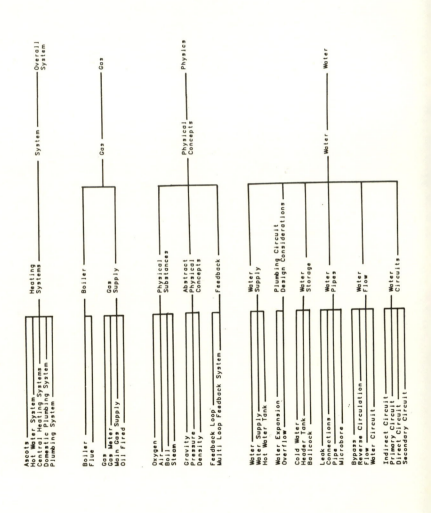

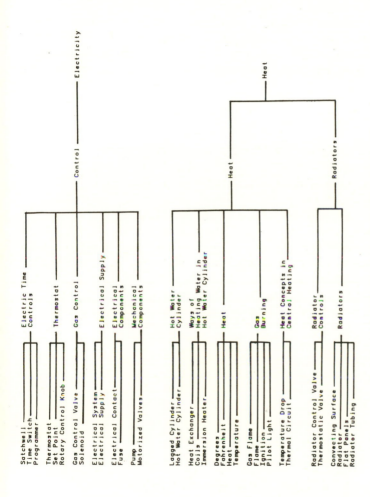

FIGURE 1. Hierarchy of concepts from card-sort task.

(phenomenal) realism of this division is supported by Minsky (1985), who speculates that (conventional) thought processes are based on "object-symbols representing things [that] often correspond to nouns. Our minds tend to describe every situation, real or mental, in terms of separate object-things and the relations between them" (Minsky, 1985, p. 132). In the philosophy of object-oriented programming (see Morgan, 1981), domain knowledge in the form of data structures is distinguished from applicable control structures (e.g., Steels, 1984; van Releghem, 1984). Our approach allows objectified domain relations to be represented declaratively but implies nothing about their procedural interpretation.

2.2. STRUCTURE ELICITATION

The second phase of this approach is to elicit structural criteria that the expert can use to organize the chosen domain concepts. This structure, assumed to derive from familiarity with the concepts, should reflect the groupings that the expert finds convenient. To the extent to which there is a sensible interpretation of this structure, this allows the knowledge base to be efficiently managed, both for the expert and for the knowledge engineer.

Several techniques exist in both psychological and technical literature that elicit conceptual structures, and some exemplary paradigms are described in Puff (1982). In this section we consider three in particular, the card-sort method, multidimensional scaling (MDS), and repertory grid.

It is convenient to distinguish grain size in the structuring of knowledge, for different techniques may be applicable to each. In this section we particularly distinguish between (1) having a global organization of the domain's major divisions and knowing which concepts properly belong to each subarea and (2) the detailed differentiations an expert makes among a few closely related things in a specialized subarea.

2.2.1. The Card-Sort Method

This refers to a family of techniques of which the method described below is a typical example. Card-sort methods have been tried using problems from the domains of physics (Chi *et al.*, 1981), mathematics (Schoenfeld and Herrmann, 1982), and computing (Weiser and Shertz, 1984). The procedure followed in the present domain was as follows.

First, the 75 concepts were typed on small individual index cards and a large table was cleared, upon which these were spread out at random. The expert was told to group together the concepts into as many small groups as possible. Any group remaining divisible had to be split, while retaining more than one element in each, and there had to be a rationale behind the grouping. The expert's spontaneous strategy for this was to form slightly larger groups first and then to split those. A think-aloud protocol was recorded during this phase, which lasted 28 minutes, and provided 25 groups. A free-recall task, in which the expert was asked to recall as many of the concepts as possible in 3 minutes, was then interpolated. This is a common procedure in psychology and was designed both to interfere with memory for the larger groups that had been formed during the first phase and to reveal any systematic retrieval strategies.

The expert was then asked to label each of the 25 groups, and then to amalgamate them into slightly larger groups, which themselves were relabeled, thinking aloud the while. This was iterated until the expert felt the groups could not be amalgamated further, which took 10 minutes. In practice, the iterations were not as discrete as intended, but this did not matter since the relevant information was recorded on tape. The recorded protocol indicated the sorts of decision criteria being considered, and was rich in propositional information, such as "Well, *pipes* contain water and so does a *header tank*, so I could group those two together. . . ."

Using think-aloud to record as much information as possible seems a good idea, provided the expert is agreeable. A recording can be an *aide-mémoire* to the knowledge engineer during subsequent analysis, but the information that recordings contain may not be easy to represent formally. We found that the simultaneous protocols recorded during this and other tasks did not provide information that could be easily represented, but they provided incidental help to the knowledge engineer in understanding the domain. The methodology of think-aloud protocols is covered in Ericsson and Simon (1984).

One strength of these methods is that experts can adapt them to their own personal style under more relaxed conditions than in many traditional psychological experiments. Under nonexperimental conditions there is plenty of scope for constructive intervention by the knowledge engineer. Work in progress with experts in other domains seems to bear out this assertion.

The outcome of this was a six-level hierarchical organization of the concepts in which the conceptual subareas of gas, water, electricity, and heat were dominant subtrees. This is shown in Figure 1. One lesson learned from this, however, was that there was a variety of conceivable levels of abstraction among the original 75 concepts, so such concepts as heat and gas, which were labels for groups of concepts at higher levels, were also concepts at the bottom level along with fuses and valves. This is not necessarily bad; the same word can describe a concept at different levels (e.g., the different senses of the word *gas*, which refers both to the particular stuff in the pipes and to an abstract physical medium), but this illustrates some problems of having a single definition per lexical item.

A related problem is that some concepts naturally belong in more than one group, and the strict hierarchical format precludes that. Some of the information about candidate groups is revealed in the protocol— for instance, the agonizing about the eventual placement of "pipes"— but in such cases it might be better to write out a duplicate card for the concept in question. The neatness of the simple tree structure then of course is lost, and the move is toward a richer, tangled hierarchy, or a net representation. In cases where a strict tree is unrealistic the card-sort organization may have little more than heuristic value, in giving an approximate overall organization, but in domains or subdomains that have a natural hierarchical structure, the method would be expected to reveal this.

Card-sort methods are likely to be adaptable to a range of applications. Sorting is a task people find natural and easy, and not just concepts, but pictures, sentences, or domain problems may be used as stimuli. The technique described by Cancian (1975) for eliciting the norms of a community by sorting familiar propositions is untried in expert communities as yet, but it looks very promising.

The utility of the technique in the present domain was that it identified rational subsystems and their attendant concepts, together with the principles or higher-order concepts that united the 75 original concepts at different levels of abstraction. Such a structure suggests a way to incorporate new concepts into the knowledge base.

2.2.2. Multidimensional Scaling

Multidimensional scaling (MDS) refers to a class of procedures for extracting structure from a matrix of data. These data are typically measures of relatedness among a set of objects whose underlying dimensions of classification are not well known, but which are presumed to vary along an interpretable number of dimensions. Kruskal and Wish (1978) indicate several sources of data suitable for analysis using MDS.

In the typical procedure, each object is compared with all others and some estimate of their similarity is given. With a spatial metaphor to represent similarity, the objects are scaled in a chosen number of dimensions, delivering a global picture of the space in which the objects lie.

From the output solution an interpretation can be offered as to the nature of the dimensions that differentiate the objects' location. The technique works best when the objects (in this case, domain concepts) are preselected so that rating their similarity is meaningful. These objects should be representative of the larger domain from which they are selected, and should form a fairly uniform set without including obviously anomalous items. This is so that they will be rated on a similar basis. Exemplary applications include differentiating flavors of cola drinks (Schiffman *et al.*, 1981) and color naming (Heider and Olivier, 1972). For a useful set of design considerations see Null (1980); for detail on the methods themselves see the monograph by Kruskal and Wish (1978) or the book by Schiffman *et al.* (1981).

We wanted to adapt the basic similarity ratings method of acquiring data suitable for MDS analysis to provide a knowledge-elicitation task that would deliver "contentful" domain knowledge as well as information about its structure. Although MDS is appropriate in scaling compared objects presumed to vary along only a few dimensions, in the procedure described below we violated this requirement. In an attempt to get a global picture of domain's underpinnings, we chose a maximally heterogeneous set, i.e., a set of objects that differed from one another in many respects.

Twenty-five concepts were taken, one from each of the groups at the bottom level of the card-sort hierarchy (Figure 1), and we performed a "reference ranking" task on these. In this task the expert had to take one of the 25 concepts to use as a reference and rank the remainder in order of similarity to this reference. Concepts deemed meaningless to compare were ignored. This was repeated until all 25 had been used as references. A think-aloud protocol was recorded during this. The task took over 2 hours and the expert required several breaks, finding the task very difficult. This difficulty was due to the very heterogeneity of the concepts because there were so many criteria by which things might be compared. The following is an example of the sort of dilemma the expert faced when considering the reference card *"boiler"*:

> *"boilers* and *hot water cylinders* both contain water,
> but *boilers* and *immersion heaters* both heat water."

Thus, the problem becomes to decide which is more important, heating or containing water. The original intentions had been (1) for the act of comparing, to bring into juxtaposition all 25 concepts so that their shared properties could be identified, and thus (2) to capture the knowledge-based components of such decisions, including the relative importance of "heating" versus "containing" water, but the scientist found it too demanding. In a similar procedure, which we describe later, much of this cognitive effort was reduced.

Using reference ranking, then, as a setting for a task that makes heavy demands on the expert's knowledge base has some practical problems, but the actual structure that emerged from a scaling of the data may have vindicated the technique, as described below.

Analysis of the matrix produced by the reference-ranking task was done using the ALSCAL method (Takane *et al.*, 1977), which provided solutions in up to four dimensions. The three-dimensional solution seemed the optimal analysis of the domain, and when this was plotted out, most of the 25 concepts clustered together in quite an intuitively satisfying manner. These clusters suggested an interpretation for the dimensions that confirmed the subareas suggested by the card sort; i.e., some concepts formed a "gas" cluster, others a "water" cluster, but this time the higher-order concept labels of "routing" and "control" emerged, which had been distributed across the original hierarchy. This suggests that MDS can be used to confirm that an elicited conceptual structure is based on enduring rather than arbitrary distinctions. Because there is quantitative information not present in the card sort, cluster analysis (Everitt, 1974) can supplement the technique to establish groupings within dimensions. This means in practice that MDS can also provide a complementary view to the hierarchy using "cross-sectional" information on similarity to capture important pervasive aspects, such as control and routing.

This three-dimensional solution was plotted as a cardboard model and shown to the expert, who reacted by saying that while some clusters of concepts were satisfying, others were in a surprising position, and how, for instance, *this* concept had more to do with *control* than suggested. The expert clearly enjoyed having a tangible representation of the domain to talk around, which suggests that an MDS solution with the "right" basic structure can be used as a conversation piece to elicit more detail.

While MDS is probably best left to its forte of structuring a stimulus set of low dimensionality, one recommendation from this study is that reference ranking can provide a knowledge-intensive activity to deliver copious amounts of information. However, the task may be unsuitably difficult when used on concepts seen as varying in too many dimensions, too few of which are common to all. However, the structure that emerges from an MDS solution may both confirm and complement that from other techniques, and the resultant solution provides a shared and discussable externalization of the expert's knowledge of the concepts' similarities, a possible alternative to rapid prototyping in getting a feel for a domain.

2.2.3. Repertory Grid Technique

An alternative to MDS in eliciting dimensions that distinguish objects is the repertory grid technique originally attributable to Kelly (1955) and described in detail by Fransella and Bannister (1977). This method has been applied in the expert systems area by Shaw and Gaines (1983) and by Boose (1984). In the traditional method three elements (in this case domain concepts) are presented and the expert is asked to pick the odd one out, naming a dimension such that the odd one is at one pole and the other two form the contrast pole. The remaining objects are rated along this dimension. This is repeated until all objects are distinct in multidimensional space. The resultant rating grid can then be analyzed, typically using cluster analysis.

Repertory grid has at least three important differences from MDS. First, the number of distinctions (dimensions) yielded by repertory grid is driven by the nature of the technique, while in MDS the dimensionality can be mathematically optimized. However, the raw grid can always be scaled or factor-analyzed afterwards if desired. Second, repertory grid requires the informant throughout to name the dimensions, while in MDS the naming is left until afterwards. Third, because of the constraints indicated above on the MDS stimulus set there is more freedom of stimulus choice with the repertory grid.

The implications of these differences are that MDS allows averaging and statistical comparisons across a number of experts, while repertory grid is more suitable for modeling a particular individual. Furthermore, the repertory grid method requires an elicitation session involving both informant and knowledge engineer, so that an interpretation of idiosyncratic labels can be agreed at the time. However, data suitable for MDS analysis might already exist and neither party need be involved until an MDS solution requiring interpretation is required. Finally, verbal labels are required throughout repertory grid elicitation, and this can help to develop a language to describe the distinctions the expert can make. This is particularly true for pictorial or other perceptual stimuli. In MDS, solutions of high dimensionality are sometimes difficult to interpret, and the labels for the dimensions may not be obvious. On the other hand sometimes the dimensions arising from a repertory grid elicitation are not applicable to the whole set of elements.

A feature of both methods is that while they may elicit structures capable of making real distinctions, these may not be commonly agreed terminology within the expert community, although they capture the criteria a particular expert really uses. In any case, the emergent structure should be validated by comparison with other techniques and/or experts if for public consumption. These techniques are particularly promising when experts can detect subtle nuances that differentiate concepts but cannot articulate the criteria by which they decide.

We wished to explore in particular some different aspects of control operating in the central heating domain, since this notion had been distributed across the card-sort tree. For this, the concepts pertaining to control in the original 75 were supplemented by others taken from a book on the subject (Crabtree, 1979), to give a total of 49 concepts. We decided to select a subset from this so that concepts of the same natural type could validly be compared. Identifying these types was done intuitively by the expert; we know of no formal way to do this in general. Four *ad hoc* categories seemed to apply to the concepts: physical notions (e.g., gravity), components (e.g., pump), subcomponents (e.g., accelerator heater on thermostat), and roles (e.g., room thermostat vs. boiler thermostat). It was decided to compare concepts in the sets of components and roles, with a total of 23 concepts.

With the triad method described above, the grid elicitation took 1½ hours and produced nine distinguishing constructs. For instance, taking the three items "gas control valve," "radiator control valve," and "pump" indicated that "radiator control valve" was different because its operation was under direct human control, while the others worked automatically. This produced the construct ("presence vs. absence of a parameter set by householder"), and each concept had a binary value on this. Three of these nine distinctions required values on a 7-point scale (e.g., "frequency of adjustment by householder"), while the rest were naturally categorical (e.g., temperature relevant vs. irrelevant) and for which a binary scale sufficed. For analysis purposes the three scalar dimensions were converted to binary ones by performing a median split on them. This lost some of the range information in the raw grid, but it was a conservative way to reduce sensitivity to variance.

The processed grid was analyzed by the use of hierarchical cluster analysis. This analysis confirmed prior intuitions, such as the VALVES forming a recognizable cluster, showing that they tended to differ from one another by their values on only one or two dimensions. However, besides confirming obvious groupings, this suggested other clusters, such as an "overriding" cluster that involved concepts from apparently different groups, i.e., thermostats, switches, and the day-omission device. One particularly elegant cluster was the threesome of FUSE, STOP-

COCK, and FUSED ISOLATOR, which each prevent some flow in the system. Clustering on the constructs was not profitable in this case, merely confirming some obvious expectations.

In the raw rating grid, each concept had a unique profile on the construct set. It would be straightforward to represent this profile as a property list for each concept. A more efficient way might be to extract common properties for particular items to inherit from a conceptual prototype, and to code only their particular differences at the object level. However, rather than dwell on particular details of how this might be formally represented, the point is that the relevant information is available to support a variety of implementation schemes, without much distortion.

In summary, then, repertory grid can elicit a vocabulary of criteria that the expert uses to differentiate among domain concepts. The profile of each concept on these distinctions is also elicited by the technique, which can then be analyzed to suggest groupings of concepts by their common properties. This is particularly useful when several domain concepts are closely related.

2.3. STRUCTURE REPRESENTATION

There is a respectable tradition throughout associationist psychology and particularly in semantic memory work of using the network representation. It has become a pervasive representation in cognitive science. For a critical review of semantic networks see Johnson-Laird et al. (1984). We chose to represent the concepts in a net for the following reasons.

1. As a declarative representation of domain relations there is no procedural knowledge necessarily implied by the formalism. We consider this important if our approach to elicitation is to be followed. This is in line with the basic architectural assumption of Anderson's ACT model of cognition (Anderson, 1983), in which separately held production systems operate on a declarative base. While a network is ideal for establishing the intensional relations among domain concepts, it has no necessary representation of, or commitment to, any "outside" world. If expert systems cannot "be" in the world in the same sense as humans can, their role will remain as assistants for those with that power.

2. A net can be easily elaborated or modified by adding or deleting links among concepts, important both for adaptive knowledge acquisition and for the practicalities of implementation. We make the assumption that expert knowledge consists not just in having more concepts explicitly represented than has someone naive but that an expert's rep-

resentation is much richer because more relations are formed among concepts. The network formalism is sufficiently powerful to represent these. (For a discussion of the power of networks again see Johnson-Laird *et al.,* 1984.) Although networks can have the power of a Universal Turing machine, this renders them empirically vacuous (Johnson-Laird *et al.,* 1984, p. 305). However, this very representational power seems desirable in a knowledge base to which meaning is imposed through interpretive processes.

3. While a multidimensional solution gives a geometrical metaphor for conceptualization, specific pairwise relations may be distorted as the scaling attempts to find a best fit. A network model preserves these relationships at the expense of the global dimensional picture; thus, a network description can completement the overall structure with local organization (Schvaneveldt *et al.,* 1984). In the next section we describe how such a model was constructed.

2.3.1. *A Network Model*

To collect information relevant to forming a network of the domain concepts we used the following method.

First, we took the original set of 25 concepts back to the expert, who was asked to sort them by considering one concept as reference, and then each of the others in turn. If there was some valid relationship between the current concept and the reference, it was placed in one pile; if not, it was discarded; and any dubious ones were placed in a third pile. The expert was able to do this very quickly. The next phase was to array the relatable concepts along a scale from 0 to 100 marked at the side of the table. The expert moved the cards around until content with the ordering and relative distance between the concepts; the values were then simply read off the scale and entered in a data matrix as before. The following benchmarks were used as guidance: Values from 50 to 99 were reserved for strongly related concepts, 20 to 49 for reasonable but not striking relations, and 1 to 19 when it was hard work to contrive a connection, or the connection was seen as tenuous. The procedure was repeated until all concepts had been used as references. This method took slightly longer than the original reference ranking, but the expert found the procedure much easier. This was because the presorting cut down the number of concepts to consider, and the external scale made the estimation of numbers more tangible. If a full rather than a half matrix is elicited, measures of reliability of ratings can be derived.

The analysis of this proximity matrix was done using the PATH-FINDER program of Schvaneveldt *et al.* (1985). This forms a network where the nodes are the rated concepts, and weighted links represent the proximities. Based on the original data, the algorithm forms a link between concepts A and B if, and only if, that link represents the shortest path between those two concepts. If it is shorter to go from A to B via C, no direct link will be formed between A and B. Two parameters allow networks of arbitrary complexity to be formed—one determines the maximum number of nodes to consider in path formation (the L parameter), while the other is the Minkowski distance measure in multidimensional space (the R parameter).

Before subjecting the data to the program, the matrix was transformed as follows. First, the similarity ratings were subtracted from 100 to give distances, and then the matrix was made symmetric by taking the minimum of cells (i,j) and (j,i) where the two ratings differed and putting this value into both cells. Taking the minimum rather than the mean of the two values was an arbitrary decision since we know of no reason to assume one criterion rather than another. Although asymmetries in distance between two concepts can be psychologically meaningful (Tversky, 1977; Tversky and Gati, 1978) and PATHFINDER allows for this, we did not want to include such information at this stage. This was because to do so might artificially overemphasize the actual numerical ratings when it seems more likely that any perceived asymmetries are highly context-specific and for most intents and purposes the similarity between A and B is the same as that between B and A.

Networks were plotted for different values of the L parameter, with R set to be infinity, which is appropriate for ordinal data. The increasing values of L represented the decrease in complexity as links dropped out with each iteration, stopping when the minimal network was achieved. The network for L = 5, shown in Figure 2, has 31 links. The number of links dropped from 44 to 30 as L increased, with R set at infinity. The link weights have been omitted from the diagram and are not discussed here.

From Figure 2 it can be seen that the domain has a clear conceptual organization. The subdomain of "plumbing" concepts is represented in the top left corner, with the "gas" concepts below them. The electrical aspects are shown in the top right corner, while the main cluster of essential central heating concepts is in the center. Peripheral but relevant concepts are included, depending from their nearest associate. Some of these may serve as hooks out to related domains of expertise.

With only a few anomalous links, this network can be interpreted directly. By a decrease in the value of the L parameter, other links can be formed increasing the complexity, and ultimately including all relatable pairs, as specified in the original rating matrix. If, as expertise develops,

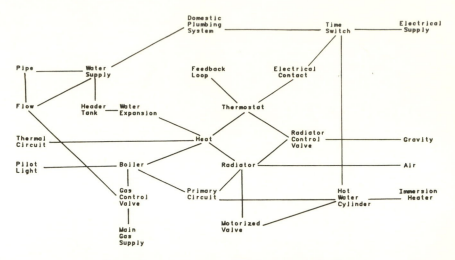

FIGURE 2. PATHFINDER network from proximity data.

more relationships are indeed formed among existing concepts, this would provide one measure by which to assess the growth of knowledge. What PATHFINDER offers is a core organization from which to elaborate a weighted network of arbitrary size.

The semantics of this organization are not implied by the network since the links do not necessarily represent a single semantic relationship, but a conceptual proximity. In the next section we describe how this network was used to guide elicitation of a set of domain propositions.

2.4. DEVELOPING THE REPRESENTATION

One way to take the network further is to elaborate the particular set of concepts to include their characteristic properties and distinctions and to link those into the structure. In this way we locally expand subdomains of interest since the network as it stands is impoverished in its restriction to a schematic representation of an overall domain picture.

At some point, however, the system must represent information about the relationships among its concepts (i.e., the labels for the arcs) as distinct from the procedural interpretation of those relational labels. In this section we show how the network can be used to guide elicitation of such relationships to develop a database of propositions.

Extracting propositional information from protocols can be both time-consuming and arbitrary, and the subsequent formal representation can be problematic. For instance, a given natural language explanation may have the following phrase:

"then burning gas heats the water in the boiler . . . "

and any number of possible propositions, both valid and invalid, may be imagined from this, such as:

"gas burns"; "gas heats water"; "gas is in boiler . . . "

from which it is clear that unless the knowledge engineer already knows enough about the domain to verify them anyway, the real intention may be missed, and errors of both omission and commission may be made.

Here we propose a method for direct elicitation of relevant propositional knowledge that can directly be encoded as a PROLOG-like database, while retaining the network structure as an equivalent pictorial alternative. These "facts" can be recruited as appropriate for a whole range of knowledge-based tasks, from design through diagnosis to explanation. However, here we say nothing about the metaknowledge assumed responsible for directing such recruitment.

The basic method used to elicit the specific relationships between concepts was simply to use the matrix of proximity ratings (equivalent to the elaborated network) and, for each pair of concepts identified by the expert as relatable, to ask what that relationship was. This task took 2 hours, during which the expert recorded a short one-predicate sentence for each pair, apart from a few that were identified as indirect relationships. Variations on this method might include taping and transcribing, or the knowledge engineer typing the spoken predicates into a file during the task. The basic task is trivial to automate, since the relevant information can be held in a stored matrix and presented as concept pairs on a screen.

The task produced 248 propositional relationships among the 24 core concepts, although 1 concept (thermal circuit) was dropped because the expert claimed it was used inconsistently in the original tutorial. Some propositions included more than 2 concepts. This number was effectively reduced to around 124 owing to symmetry. Many of the relationships were dependent or componential [e.g., part of (radiator, primary circuit)]; others involved dynamic aspects between concepts [e.g., feeds (water supply, header tank); warms (radiator, air)]. Sometimes relations were not so direct—the elicited relationship between *boiler* and *header tank* was as follows:

"*boiler* supplies *heat* [that] causes
        water expansion [that] requires *header tank*,"

which indicates the remote relationship of "necessitates" between those concepts.

The pairwise relationships represented in this complex relationship were elicited individually for the component pairs of concepts. Incidentally, this chain is also represented in the illustrated network. Although pairwise information could possibly be derived by analyzing chains that naturally occurred in protocols, it is preferable rather to synthesize the chains systematically, perhaps using the network as a guide. This is because more than one relationship may hold between pairs of concepts, but in a chain of causality only one is likely to be considered. For instance, "radiators warm air," but also "radiators may contain air."

Some predicates are themselves complex and require elaboration—for instance, causality and control, which are attributed in a number of different senses. Evidently the semantics of such relational terms requires more specification. Differentiating the nature of "control" is fairly straightforward in this limited domain, and slotting in extra arguments or having separate predicates may suffice, depending on how the profile of information from the repertory grid is implemented—for example

controls (time switch, boiler, on–off,
$>=$ once daily, electrically, . . .)
controls (rad control valve, room temp, continuous,
$<$once daily, thermostatically, . . .)

A taxonomy of relational terms, together with a calculus specifying their valid composition, would seem desirable. For a circumscribed domain this may be possible, given that only 15 predicates account for all of the propositions, and 6 of those account for over two-thirds of the total. We have not tackled this problem yet; for possibly relevant work in this area see Chaffin and Herrmann (1984).

3. USING THE KNOWLEDGE BASE

In our view of knowledge, the set of propositions represents some of the declarative components that are recruited for a variety of tasks. In this section we show how the database of propositions can provide information relevant to several different queries. If the knowledge base is formulated with an expert system in mind, relevant procedural knowledge must be considered and elicited using appropriate techniques, and the great problem of how experts use their knowledge is not to be minimized. These procedures will change with the intended purposes of the system, and they are analogous to specific recipes applied to (propositional) ingredients.

However, representing the declarative knowledge in its own right may be useful for other knowledge-based applications, such as the archiving of rare expertise or the construction of training manuals. Simply having a base of knowledge that is independent of a single imposed rule context can present facts relevant to explanation, design, or decision tasks, thus serving as an informed consultant or external memory to a human expert.

We coded the propositions as a (PROLOG) database that was then queried in a variety of ways, to illustrate that knowledge relevant to producing an answer was represented therein. Since there are a finite number of concepts represented here, any evaluation is of necessity more illustrative than complete.

The first test was to find out about the primary circuit. Simple pattern matching using the predicate "part of" indicated that it included a boiler, an optional number of motorized valves and radiator control valves, hot water cylinder, pipes, and radiators. Had PUMP been in the original set of 25 concepts, this would have completed the set of components. Had the concept of PUMP never been elicited in the first place, presenting this list to the expert and asking if there was anything missing might be one method to expand the knowledge base.

Seeking more information about the primary circuit retrieved the facts that the header tank supplies it (with water), that flow and water expansion happen in the circuit, that it carries and distributes heat, that gravity causes flow in it, and that the boiler heats the water in it. The primary circuit itself is a conceptual component of the domestic plumbing system. It is affected by thermostatic control and it should not contain air.

One can imagine this information being used in a variety of tasks from design to explanation. A similar exercise could be performed for other concepts.

Retrieval can also be done on predicates—for instance, trying to discover what the system's requirements might be. The following examples illustrate some bindings to the match "?—requires (X,Y)."

immersion heater	electric supply
motorized valve	electric supply
water expansion	header tank
hot water cylinder	water supply
pilot light	air

This database supports questions of the form "What are the electrical components of the system?" assuming this can readily be translated into "requires (X, electric supply)."

Causal interdependencies in the domain can be propagated through conceivable paths to allow arbitrary chains of indefinite length to be discovered; for instance, causal connections between remote concepts A and C can be found by the recursive query "leads to":

[causes (a,b).

   :

   :

causes (b,c).   ]
leads to (A,C) *if* causes (A,C) *or*
                     (causes (A,B) *and* leads to (B,C)).

Since causality is multifaceted, the label "causes" may require widening, to embrace predicates such as "controls," "produces," etc. This is an implementation detail as much as a theoretical one. Examples of this from the present database show that there is a declared conceivable sequence of enablement and control from the electrical supply through the time switch to a set of components under time switch control. Some of these components (e.g., radiator control valve) themselves control radiators and ultimately room air temperature.

Without representing any notions of what constitutes valid transitivities among semantic relationships, or having any other constraints on the composition of elementary propositions, such a procedure might be dangerous. However, rudimentary information supporting construction of possible world models is available in the database, and the constraints can be imposed at a later stage.

Information about dual control of components and feedback loops can also be discovered in the database. For instance, the time switch *and* a gas control valve *and* a thermostat operate together to control the boiler, while the *radiator control valve* affects the *radiator's* effect on *room air temperature*, which affects the *thermostatic control*, which affects the *radiator control valve*.

4. FUTURE RESEARCH

Our concern in this work has been the elicitation of declarative knowledge capable of supporting a variety of eventualities but saying little about how any particular application may make use of that knowledge. Using techniques appropriate to capturing procedural aspects of expert knowledge would be the logical next stage of this research, embodying such knowledge probably in a set of task-oriented production systems. Such production systems would have to identify relevant information for a given problem and recruit facts relevant to its solution. Task protocol analysis (Ericsson and Simon, 1984) is one suggested technique for capturing such knowledge.

Since there appears to be no *a priori* way to taxonomize all possible problems in a domain, a set of procedures operating on this declarative base must be limited in some way to cover a useful range of contingency classes. The problem-sorting techniques described above can deliver a classificatory structure for typical problems in a domain. The CENTAUR system of Aikins (1983), in which procedural information pertaining to prototypical situations is separately held, provides one possible model here.

On the techniques themselves, more research could be done to try to establish their utility, but their true value will best be shown through practice. Also, the manner in which the techniques have been presented does not necessarily imply that they must be conducted as a "scientific" experiment; the view we have of them is rather of their being adaptable, informal, and cooperative, and in all probability, practicing knowledge engineers do similar things already. Perhaps, however, our explorations suggest a place for these and similar methods in the knowledge engineer's toolbox.

5. GUIDELINES SUMMARY

Tutorial Interview and Related Methods

Strengths:
- Gives knowledge engineer orientation to domain
- Generates a lot of relevant material cheaply and in a natural manner
- Little demand on expert other than time

Weaknesses:
- Incomplete and arbitrary coverage
- Requires training and/or social skills to be done properly
- Burden of representation and interpretation on knowledge engineer

Rule of thumb:
- Use early to get terms of reference and possible framework

- If interviewing comes naturally to both parties, then interview methods may be fruitful

Card Sort

Strengths:
- Gives clusters of concepts meaningful to expert
- Indicates possible uniting principles across abstraction levels
- Provides hierarchical organization, useful in indexing and placing new concepts
- Splits large domain into manageable subareas
- Easy for people to do, wide range of application

Weaknesses:
- Strict hierarchy may be too restrictive
- Permits only one view per sort
- Some aspects may become distributed and lost by method

Rule of thumb:
- Use to reveal possible hierarchical organization and to reveal principles of that organization

Multidimensional Scaling (On Relatedness Measures)

Strengths:
- Provides global picture of similarity of domain concepts
- Indicates dimensions for distinguishing objects
- Knowledge engineer's involvement unnecessary if suitable data already exist
- Many computerized analysis methods available
- Allows comparison/averaging across expert sources

Weaknesses:
- Results may be uninterpretable or not very useful
- Supplementary analysis may be required to represent local information faithfully
- Better at delivering "structure" than "content"

Rule of thumb:
- Principled sets of objects should be used when trying to elicit criteria for differentiation
- Good in (sub)domains when words may be inadequate for describing distinctions
- Gives overall picture giving handle on domain, thus may be a useful alternative to rapid prototyping, e.g., for feasibility

Repertory Grid

Strengths:
- Captures distinctions among closely related concepts useful to the expert
- Elicits expert's personal concepts in absence of public vocabulary
- Few, if any, constraints on subject matter, e.g., can be done on perceptual and nonverbal data

Weaknesses:
- Distinctions may not be publically agreed
- Larger concept sets require more expert time

Rule of thumb:
- Use with single expert in small set of closely related concepts, especially where no agreed vocabulary already exists

Proximity Analysis (PATHFINDER)

Strengths:
- Complements MDS by retaining information on local structuring
- Outputs network representation of domain concepts
- Shows which links are likely to be meaningful, with associated strengths

Weaknesses:
- Parameter settings require tuning
- May require arbitrary estimates as input data

Rule of thumb:
- Use in reducing matrix of relatedness measures to minimal network, which gives core structure of domain

"Matrix Technique"

Strengths:
- Organizes "complete" elicitation of pairwise propositions for a set of concepts
- Fast results and easy to automate procedure
- Provides direct representation of relevant domain information

Weaknesses:
- Combinatorics prohibitive without some guidance, e.g., PATHFINDER method
- Relational terms may require explanation
- Not yet fully developed and tested

Rule of thumb: • Use systematically to elicit relationships and connections for an object-centered database

ACKNOWLEDGMENTS. I wish to thank Richard Young, who has been involved throughout. This research is supported by a SERC/Unilever cooperative award.

6. REFERENCES

Aikins, J. S. (1983). Prototypical knowledge for expert systems. *Artificial Intelligence, 20,* 163–210.

Anderson, J. R. (1983). The Architecture of cognition. London: Harvard University Press.

Boose, J. H. (1984). Personal construct theory and the transfer of human expertise. In T. O'Shea (Ed.), *ECAI-84: Advances in artificial intelligence.* Amsterdam: Elsevier, North-Holland.

Cancian, F. (1975). *What are norms?* Cambridge: Cambridge University Press.

Chaffin, R., and Herrmann, D. J. (1984). The similarity and diversity of semantic relations. *Memory and Cognition, 12,* 134–141.

Chi, M. T. H., Feltovich, P. J., and Glaser, R. (1981). Categorisation and representation of physics problems by experts and novices. *Cognitive Science, 5,* 121–152.

Crabtree, T. (1979). *Do your own central heating controls.* London: Foulsham.

Ericsson, K. A., and Simon, H. A. (1984). *Protocol analysis: Verbal reports as data.* Cambridge, Mass.: Bradford Books/MIT Press.

Everitt, B. (1974). *Cluster analysis.* SSRC reviews of current research 11. London: Heinemann Educational Books.

Fransella, F., and Bannister, D. (1977). *A manual for repertory grid technique.* London: Academic Press.

Gammack, J. G., and Young, R. M. (1985). Psychological techniques for eliciting expert knowledge. In M. A. Bramer (Ed.), *Research and development in expert systems.* Cambridge: Cambridge University Press.

Grover, M. D. (1983). A pragmatic knowledge acquisition methodology. In A. Bundy (Ed.), *Proceedings of the eighth international joint conference on artificial intelligence,* Karlsruhe, pp. 436–438.

Heider, R. E., and Olivier, D. C. (1972). The structure of the colour space in naming and memory from two languages. *Cognitive Psychology, 3,* 337–354.

Johnson-Laird, P. N., Herrmann, D. J., and Chaffin, R. (1984). Only connections: A critique of semantic networks. *Psychological Bulletin, 96,* 292–315.

Kelly, G. A. (1955). The psychology of personal constructs. New York: Norton.

Kruskal, J. B., and Wish, M. (1978). *Multidimensional scaling.* Sage University paper series on quantitative applications in the social sciences, Series No. 07-011. Beverly Hills and London: Sage.

Minsky, M. (1985). Communication with alien intelligence. *BYTE, 10*(4), 127–138.

Morgan, C. (Ed.). (1981). "Smalltalk." BYTE [Special issue], August.

Null, C. H. (1980). Design considerations for multidimensional scaling. *Behavior Research Methods and Instrumentation, 12,* 274–280.

Puff, C. R. (Ed.). (1982). *Handbook of research methods in human memory and cognition.* London: Academic Press.

Schiffman, S., Reynolds, M. L., and Young, F. W. (1981). *Introduction to multidimensional scaling.* London: Academic Press.

Schoenfeld, A. H., and Herrmann, D. J. (1982). Problem perception and knowledge structure in expert and novice mathematical problem solvers. *Journal of Experimental Psychology: Learning, Memory, and Cognition, 5,* 484–494.

Schvaneveldt, R. W., Cooke, N. M., Goldsmith, T. E., DeMaio, J. C., Breen, T. J., Durso, F. T., and Tucker, R. G. (1984). *Cognitive organization as a function of flying experience.* Report number AFHRL-TR-83-64. Williams Air Force Base, Ariz.: HQ Air Force Human Resources Laboratory.

Schvaneveldt, R. W., Durso, F. T., and Dearholt, D. W. (1985). PATHFINDER: *Scaling with network structures.* Memorandum in Computer and Cognitive Science, MCCS-85-9. Computing Research Laboratory, New Mexico State University.

Shaw, M. L. G., and Gaines, B. R. (1983). A computer aid to knowledge engineering. In J. Fox (Ed.), *Proceedings of the third BCS conference on expert systems,* Cambridge, pp. 263–271.

Steels, L. (1984). Object-oriented knowledge representation in KRS. In T. O'Shea (Ed.), *ECAI-84: Advances in artificial intelligence.* Amsterdam: Elsevier, North-Holland.

Takane, Y., Young, F. W., and de Leeuw, J. (1977). Nonmetric individual differences multidimensional scaling: An alternating least squares method with optimal scaling features. *Psychometrika, 42,* 7–67.

Tversky, A. (1977). Features of similarity. *Psychological Review, 84,* 327–352.

Tversky, A., and Gati, I. (1978). Studies of similarity. In E. Rosch and B. B. Lloyd. *Cognition and categorisation.* Hillsdale, N.J.: Erlbaum.

van Releghem, E. (1984). Separating control knowledge from domain knowledge. In T. O'Shea (Ed.), *ECAI-84: Advances in artificial intelligence.* Amsterdam: Elsevier, North-Holland.

Weiser, M., and Shertz, J. (1984). Programming problem representation in novice and expert programmers. *International Journal of Man-Machine Studies, 19,* 391–398.

Wright, P. (1971). Writing to be understood: Why use sentences? *Applied Ergonomics, 24,* 207–209.

Wright, P. (1974, January). For sharp, hard-hitting reports: Alternatives to prose. *Machine Design.*

8

Role of Induction in Knowledge Elicitation

ANNA HART

1. INTRODUCTION

There are many types of knowledge. Knowledge is not simply a collection of facts and rules that are learned easily. An expert augments documented facts and procedures with knowledge gleaned from years of experience in his particular field. He needs to practice to become skillful, using rules of thumb or heuristics, learning which rules work and when they work. He develops judgment, insight, and informed opinions. It is the quality of this undocumented knowledge that determines his level of expertise. The way in which this process takes place is by no means fully understood, and so it is hardly surprising that the subsequent process of knowledge elicitation is very difficult (Kidd and Welbank, 1984).

In systems analysis the analyst asks about procedures or rules that are followed, together with data about volume and frequency. Much of the information that is not known can, except for the case of predicting trends, be found by interviewing, observation, or sampling. Poor analysis is usually caused by either failing to ask a question or misunderstanding the answer. In knowledge elicitation the problem is far more complex. The expert may be able to tell you his decision or diagnosis, but not the details of the procedures he used. He may use knowledge without even being aware that he has that knowledge. It is very likely that he has

ANNA HART • Lancashire Polytechnic, Preston PR1 2TQ, England.

never been required to formulate his decision making, and he could have many assumptions or beliefs that have not been stated explicitly. An expert can be surprised and even alarmed when the simple consequences of these assumptions are pointed out (Jackson, 1985), and consequently he may be reluctant to admit to them. In contrast, if asked which factors he takes into consideration, he may list those he thinks he ought to use, which will not necessarily be the same as those he does use. This is not deliberate deception; it is because the expert will have learned a lot of his knowledge by experience, and he may use it without consciously being aware of the explicit details. The process of closely questioning the expert can interfere with his own perception of what he does.

In summary: (1) An expert finds it hard to give detailed descriptions of his knowledge and how he uses it. It is unlikely that he has been required to do this before. (2) The process of knowledge elicitation can alter the expert's view of what he does.

2. INDUCTION

2.1. General Principles

In many cases the expert will find it easier to describe cases that are documented, or to give examples of different types of decisions. These examples consist of the decisions and the factors involved in the decisions, without the details of how he assessed different evidence and resolved conflicts in order to reach his decisions. Such sets of examples form the basis for inductive learning. An induction program might be able to induce rules from the examples: rules that the expert himself might not be able to formulate.

In deductive learning we are given a rule that is true in general, and we deduce that it applies in specific cases. For example, suppose we are told that

In country X all citizens receive a state pension from the age of 55 years.

If we are then told that

Mr. Bloggs is a citizen of X aged 57 years,

then we deduce that

Mr. Bloggs is receiving a state pension.

If the original rule is true then the deduction will be true.

Induction works the other way round: We are given specific examples and we induce a general rule. Suppose we do not know the rule for entitlement to a state pension in country X, but that we are given sample data about a set of citizens; then we can "guess" the age rule. In the case where ages of citizens in receipt of a pension were 58, 61, 62, and 78, and ages of those not receiving a pension were 23, 42, and 49, we might induce that the age of entitlement was 50. In fact, any value between 50 and 57 could be justified, and this range obviously includes the correct value of 55. Notice that the induced rule depends on both the algorithm we are using and the particular example set we had. There is no guarantee that the induced rule is correct, but if the algorithm is "efficient," and the example set "informative," then we would expect the rule to be "good." The terms in this statement have not been defined; they are necessarily fuzzy.

Unfortunately, the quality of the induced rules can vary even more. If we did not know that it was age that determined entitlement, then we might have data describing some other attribute of citizens. To consider an extreme case, we might have information about citizens' hair. If citizens were classified as one of bald, white, gray, dark, or fair, then, ignoring the problems of actually classifying certain cases, we might induce a rule that worked reasonably well for the examples. This would be due to the fact that older people, in receipt of a pension, will tend to fall in the first three categories. We would expect the rule to be poor at predicting entitlement in general, although it might work very well for our selected example set.

Induction is a subject of controversy. Its fiercest defenders allege that it will solve not only problems of knowledge elicitation (Michie, 1985) but most of the world's problems too (Michie and Johnston, 1985).

Others are less optimistic (Fox, 1984) or even dismissive. Several people have designed algorithms, e.g., Buchanan, Hayes-Roth, Winston, and Michalski (Dieterrich and Michalski, 1981), but one that is used in some commercial software, including expert system shells, is Quinlan's ID3 algorithm (Quinlan, 1979). The rest of this chapter is concerned, in the main, with an evaluation of one implementation of this particular algorithm.

2.2. The ID3 Algorithm

Implementations of ID3 vary, but the principle is that the algorithm induces a decision tree of rules from a bank, or training set, of examples. The examples consist of classes and attributes. The class is the decision of the expert, and the attributes are the characteristics or measurements of the examples that the expert used to reach his decision. The tree is induced from the training set and is generally used for one of two purposes: (1) to explain the underlying pattern and effects of the attributes, (2) to predict outcomes for examples not explicitly in the training set. In commercial literature (2) is more usually advertised, but (1) is equally important, and a careful discussion of (1) provides the basis for being able to do (2). The principles are illustrated in Figure 1. The inductive program has read through the training set of case histories of diagnoses and induced the rules. For example, if the pain is low, then the disease is not present; if the pain is medium and the patient's age is less

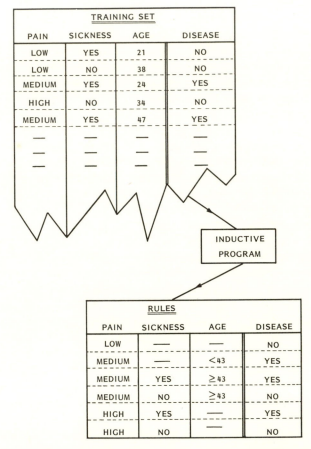

FIGURE 1. An inductive program reads in a training set of examples with attributes (Pain, Sickness, Age) and classes (Yes, No). It induces rules that apply for the training set and form the basis for the knowledge handling.

than 43, then the disease is present. The rules will give accurate results for the training set but may not be completely correct in general.

The process is very similar to that of taxonomy, and it is enlightening to read some of the taxonomists' findings because many of the problems they describe apply to induction (Gordon, 1981; Sneath and Sokal, 1973).

Attributes are of two types, either categorical or real. An attribute that is categorical will have a value that falls in one of a set of discrete, or separate, categories. For example, the attribute *color*, having possible values *black, white, blue, yellow*, is categorical. For real variables there are potentially infinitely many values, but in practice there will be no more values than the number of examples in the training set, and those values may be restricted because of the accuracy of measurement. Height and weight are real attributes. A real measurement can be coded into a categorical attribute by defining subclasses or subranges—for example *small, medium, large*—assuming that these subclassifications are sensible. The expert may know this from existing knowledge or beliefs. For example, a doctor may measure blood pressure and record it as *low, normal,* or *high.* If such groupings are not known, then the real attribute should be used. The classes are categorical values: decisions that fall into discrete types.

An induction algorithm requires the following: (1) criteria for splitting the set into successive subsets; these criteria determine the rules; (2) some criterion for stopping, i.e., deeming a node on the tree to be terminal; (3) a method of allocating the class at a terminal node.

Figure 2 illustrates these features. This is a decision tree describing the induced rules from Figure 1. We traverse the tree, depending on the values of the attributes named in the intermediate nodes, until we reach a terminal node. Reading the tree from left to right, we find that the rules are as follows: (1) If the pain is low, disease is not present. (2) If the pain is medium and age is less than 43, then disease is present. (3) If the pain is medium and age is not less than 43 and there is sickness, then disease is present.

2.2.1. Splitting

ID3, the Iterative Dichotomizer 3, was developed by Ross Quinlan in the context of chess playing (Quinlan, 1979). The data were categorical, so we shall consider those cases first. Given a subset of examples, the algorithm selects the attribute from those as yet unused, which subdivides the set in the "best" way. This process is repeated recursively on the resulting subsets. To define "best," the information statis-

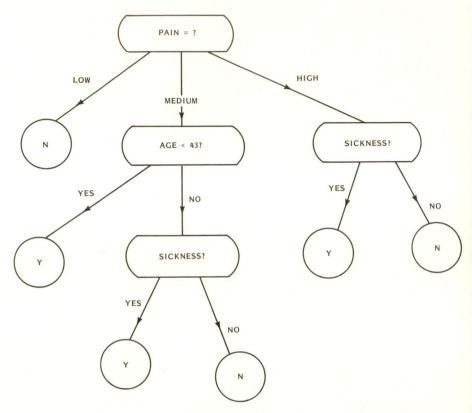

FIGURE 2. A decision tree can be used to represent rules. Intermediate nodes on the tree describe the rules, and terminal nodes (at the bottom) describe the decisions. Given the values of the attributes, we traverse the tree until we reach a terminal node.

tic (Kullback, 1967) based on Shannon's information function is calculated as follows:

Suppose that we have a subset of examples with proportion p_1 in Class 1, p_2 in Class 2, and so on where p's sum to 1. Then the information value of that set, I_0, is given by:

$$I_0 = -\Sigma\, p_i \log_2 p_i$$

Note that I_0 has a maximum value when all the p's are equal; that is, the classes are evenly distributed throughout the set. This means that there is still a lot of information in this set. I_0 is minimized to zero if one of the p's is unity and the others are zero: In this case all examples belong to one class, and there is no more information in the set.

Now if we subdivide the subset according to the values of an attribute, we shall have a number of subsets. For each of these subsets we can compute the information value. Let the information value for subset n be i_n, then the new information value I_1 is given by

$$I_1 = \Sigma \, q_n \, i_n$$

where q_n is the proportion of examples having attribute value n. I_1 will be smaller than I_0, and the difference $(I_o - I_1)$ is a measure of how well the attribute has discriminated between different classes. ID3 selects the attribute that maximizes this difference (Hart, 1985a). Consider the data in Table 1, where attributes are *color* and *size*, and the class is Y or N.

$$I_0 = -\left(\frac{17}{45} \log_2 \frac{17}{45} + \frac{28}{45} \log_2 \frac{28}{45} \right) = 0.964$$

Using attribute *color*

$$I_1 = \frac{11}{45}(0.845) + \frac{11}{45}(0.946) + \frac{23}{45}(0.886) = 0.89$$

and so

$$(I_0 - I_1) = 0.07$$

Using attribute *size*

$$I_1 = \frac{19}{45}(0.949) + \frac{26}{45}(0.706) = 0.81$$

and

$$I_0 - I_1 = 0.15$$

so *size* would be selected.

This method can be modified to cater for real attributes. It is necessary for the algorithm to define categories for a real attribute X, usually by splitting the continuum into two sets with a rule such as "X greater than 41." In practice there will be only finitely many such cutoff points to choose from, because they are determined by the examples. For example, potential cutoff points could be the midpoints between successive pairs of (ordered) observations. The cutoff point selected should

TABLE 1. ID3 Using the Information Statistic[a]

Size	Color			Totals		
	Red	Black	Green			
Big	3Y 2N	5Y 1N	4Y 4N	12Y 7N	0.949	Information given size = 0.81
Small	6N	2Y 3N	3Y 12N	5Y 21N	0.706	
	3Y 8N	7Y 4N	7Y 16N	17Y 28N		
	0.845	0.946	0.886	$I_0 = 0.96$		
	Information given color = 0.89					

[a]It calculates the information gained by knowing the value of a particular attribute (e.g., *color* or *size*) and selects the one where this gain is maximized. In this case, *size* would be chosen.

then be the one that minimizes the value of I_1, thereby identifying the "best" rule for that attribute. The difference $(I_0 - I_1)$ can then be compared in the usual way with the values for other real and categorical attributes. The cutoff point will obviously depend on the training set.

ID3 was designed to cater for problems with two classes, although it has been further modified to cope with many classes. In general, the output is more difficult to interpret if there are many classes.

2.2.2. Stopping

ID3 assumes that there are no contradictions or errors in the training set, and so continues splitting, using one attribute at a time, until the information value at a node is zero. As contradictory data (identical attributes but different classes) are not allowed, the algorithm will terminate.

2.2.3. Node Classification

Owing to the nature of the algorithm as described in 2.2.1 and 2.2.2, it is obvious that the node classification is trivially determined by the examples at that node, or is unknown if there are no examples at the node.

3. A CASE STUDY

3.1. BACKGROUND AND RATIONALE

An induction package was used to analyze the procedures carried out by an admissions tutor in a college. There were two intentions: (1) to evaluate the use of the package, and (2) to discover how the tutor worked in order to document the procedure. This had been tried, unsuccessfully, several times before. Although the development of an expert system was not a primary aim, the results of (2) enabled a simple system to be produced. It is known that other colleges are doing similar studies. The problems of selection of candidates affect industry and commerce too.

3.2. THE KNOWLEDGE DOMAIN

Each year the admissions tutor receives applications from students wishing to enroll in the department's courses. Throughout the year he does this work on his own, but in the summer vacation other staff relieve him. Previous attempts to produce guidelines had resulted in booklets of several pages mainly concerned with the pseudolegal aspects: rules about grants, details of which letters to send out and when, etc. Although these facts were cumbersome to remember, the problem experienced by other staff was more fundamental: They found it difficult to decide whether or not to offer a student a place. The expert's judgment and skill in this area was not understood by others.

This was an ideal case for induction for the following reasons:

1. The knowledge engineer was aware of the domain, the problem, and the terminology. This meant that the inductive process could take place without extensive consultations with the expert.
2. Application forms from the previous 2 years were available as a ready-made example set.
3. The expert was available and reasonably willing to cooperate.

3.3. PROCEDURES

The description of this study highlights problems and mistakes. This account should therefore be taken not as a definitive scenario of how to approach induction (guidelines appear later) but rather as a historical account of what did, and can, happen in the process. This was a relatively simple problem, and a small increase in complexity of domain knowledge tends to produce a great increase in the problems of knowledge elicitation (Feigenbaum and McCorduck, 1984). However, discussions with other knowledge engineers indicate that they have had similar experiences using induction for both simple and complex problems.

3.3.1. Initial Contact with the Expert

The knowledge engineer explained the purposes of the investigation to the expert and asked for his cooperation. Owing to the possibly sensitive nature of some of the data, the expert was reassured about the use of the forms, and he agreed to it. He also agreed to taking part in tape-recorded interviews. His initial reaction was rather dismissive: "Oh it's easy. If they've got the minimum requirements then I offer a place, otherwise I don't." This was clearly an oversimplification.

3.3.2. The Training Set

The first task was to draw up the data for a training set from the forms. This was done without consulting the expert. Of the 2 years' forms available, there were over 300 for each year. Because of the possibility that the expert might have followed different rules in different years (there was no reason to believe this), the two sets were kept separate and the training set selected from the earlier year's data. Each application form had been coded with a unique application number, and this was used to select a training set from the year's forms. It was decided to select half of the examples randomly, and to use the remainder to test the predictive powers of the induced tree. (In fact, the original algorithm by Quinlan includes the facility to do something similar, but many implementations leave this to the knowledge engineer.) The choice of half was arbitrary, and other authorities recommend a 2:1 split (Breiman et al., 1984), but there are no theoretical reasons for this. The classes were fairly easy to define:

D   Definite unconditional offer.
ID   Interview and then definite offer.
R   Reject.
IR   Interview and then reject.
P   Provisional offer—the student has to meet some requirements.
IP   Interview and then provisional offer.

Attributes were to be derived from the entries on the application forms— for example, age, sex, locality, academic qualifications, examinations to be taken.

The only possible problem seemed to be the coding of any comments made on the form by the expert. This turned out to be irrelevant: All the comments described letters that had been exchanged, reflecting the legalistic emphasis mentioned in 3.2, and also the expert's view that the decision process was simple. The only other marks were ticks against qualifications, and crosses against spelling mistakes or caveats in the reference. On the top of the form he had coded the student's location (i.e., home address) as LOCAL or REMOTE.

Using most of the data from the forms, the training set comprised over 150 examples with 15 attributes. This set was used to induce rules. However, the effective size of this set was actually much smaller. The algorithm assumes that there are no contradictions or errors in the data, and two identical examples are treated as one. This is because of the difference between two views of examples: their actual distribution in real life, and the view from the decision tree. One hundred typical examples that take exactly the same route down the decision tree are effectively one case. For the decision tree a very rare example defining a different route in the tree is another, single case. So ID3 requires many different types of cases. The distribution of examples required by the algorithm may be quite different from their actual distribution as they occur. This is difficult to judge when compiling the training set. In this study the inadequacies were highlighted in the induced tree, which appeared oversimplistic; in other instances the omissions might not be so evident.

It followed that the random selection process had not only chosen many superfluous examples, it had also omitted some of the interesting cases. A random selection will almost certainly give a typical selection of common examples. The chance that a rare, but possibly important, example will be selected is not high enough. The selection process should reflect the decision process, not the everyday occurrence of problems.

RULE   Selection of examples is not trivial.

3.3.3. Choice of Attributes

Further examination of the induced rules, particularly the order in which attributes appeared, suggested that the choice of attributes could be improved too. There had been a tendency to include too many attributes in the misguided hope that this would produce a better result. In particular, some of the attributes could be grouped, e.g., instead of itemizing all the qualifications needed to meet the minimum requirements, a single attribute, *minrequirements*, which could be true or false, would be better. The expert's marks on the forms, together with his initial statement of policy, indicated that he viewed the qualifications in this way. The fact that ID3 considers a single attribute at a time means that efficient grouping like this will improve results. Some other attributes that looked highly correlated in the data were also regrouped— e.g., general appearance of application form and quality of last page of form, age and mature/school-leaver. Taxonomists warn against the use of correlated attributes (Gordon, 1981; Sneath and Sokal, 1973). The chosen attributes should be those that are most relevant and natural in the view of the expert. The way in which the expert describes the attributes is part of his expertise.

RULE   Selection of attributes requires skill.

3.3.4. Refining the Examples

The training set and attributes were then completely reorganized. The examples were divided into the six classes and about the same number selected randomly from each, so that each class was represented equally. (An alternative procedure would be to select a fixed proportion from each class; Breiman et al., 1984.)

The quality of the training set influences the quality of the induced tree, and, although very little commercial documentation emphasizes this, much of the skill lies in the selection of examples and attributes because the package has only the examples to work on. In practice this may mean tedious reentering of examples several times.

RULE   It is likely that the example set will need refining several times before the results are satisfactory.

If the example set is chosen carefully by the expert, then the need for refinement will be smaller, but induction is still likely to identify gaps and contradictions.

3.3.5. Further Modifications

The induced tree was beginning to look sensible by this stage. This judgment was formed by the knowledge engineer on the basis of some knowledge about the process. In other words, the knowledge engineer recognized that the induced rules could match the expert's procedure. In confirmation the induced rules performed well on further examples. The first attribute selected was *minrequirements,* followed by *reference, appearance of form,* etc. However, rules at the lower end of the tree did not make much sense. The attribute *application number* appeared repeatedly. Since this number uniquely identified the forms, then a tree could be induced based entirely on this one attribute. Clearly such a tree would have little to do with the selection process, and much more to do with that specific training set. Once the "good" attributes had been used, the algorithm repeatedly selected this one, which discriminated well by chance. Taxonomists warn against such attributes (Sneath and Sokal, 1973). Since the selection process did vary according to the number of applications already received, the attribute was retained but recoded as the leftmost digit, i.e., 0, 1, 2, or 3.

RULE   Avoid attributes that are labels.

Careful inspection of the tree revealed that the only distinction between students who were interviewed and those who were not was their locality. This was a simple discovery from the data that was not recognized in the department. The examples were therefore recoded as R, D, or P—i.e., reject, definite offer, or provisional offer. This practice of anticipating results should be applied with great care, but it can be useful.

A similar dilemma arises when two examples contradict each other. The obvious solution is to introduce an extra attribute to distinguish between them. This will work perfectly well, but the result will tell you no more than what you deliberately introduced.

RULE   Beware of imposing your solution on the program.

This is particularly true while refining the example set as described earlier.

3.3.6. Evaluation of Results

The induced tree was tested with all of the unused examples and had a very good success rate of over 92%. However, this success rate must be interpreted carefully. As described earlier, many of the examples were essentially identical, and this inflated the success rate. The tree is good if it can deal with interesting or unusual cases. Here the success rate was lower.

RULE   Take care testing the results—the tree should work for hard and easy cases.

The algorithm had provided reasonable rules for the common and "easy" examples, and indicated which cases were interesting or difficult.

RULE   Induction is unlikely to answer all questions, but it may highlight interesting or difficult cases.

3.4. SUMMARY OF FINDINGS

The program had produced good rules for straightforward rejection and offers. An analysis of discrepancies in prediction indicated some areas of interest.

Assessment of Reference and Form. This refers to the referee's opinion of the candidate in terms of suitability for the course, and the neatness, correctness, completeness, and detail of the information supplied by the student. A change in the category of reference or form—e.g., *poor* altered to *fair*, or *good* to *fair*, almost invariably changed the prediction to the correct value. The assessment of these features had been done by the knowledge engineer, which was possibly a bad policy. Such judgment is obviously an important area of expertise. It was felt that this judgment could be detailed only by consultation with the expert. Induction is unlikely to help in such matters of judgment.

Mature Students. Another interesting class was students without qualifications who had definite offers. The decision tree had classified these as students aged between 21 and 41—an unrealistic rule. There were almost certainly other factors apart from age that classified them, and these factors had not been included as attributes. There were few of these examples and so further induction was unlikely to clarify the issue with any certainty. The inductive process had been useful in identifying these special and rare cases.

Induction had produced some of the existing documented rules, discovered some apparent rules of thumb from the data, and indicated problems. See Figure 3 for the final tree. Students who have the minimum requirements are given definite offers if they apply early. If they apply later, then the reference and age are taken into account. If there are examinations to be taken, then the reference, age, and quality of the form are considered. The only other cases to be considered are mature students; these are a special case. Notice how most of the attributes that appear in this tree are the ones that were changed or discussed during

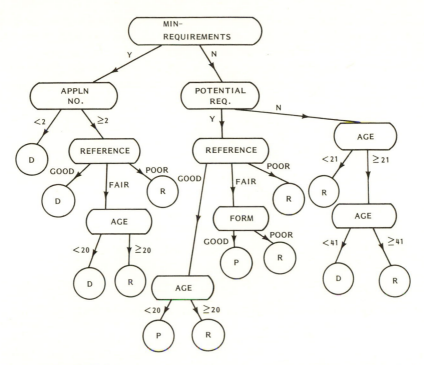

FIGURE 3. The final decision tree induced from the program. This was obtained after several refinements of the training set.

the refinement of the training set. This tree does not tackle the problem of defining the terms *good*, *fair*, and *poor*.

3.5. INTERVIEWING THE EXPERT

3.5.1. Procedure

After the production of the tree the expert was interviewed. The purpose of the interviews with the expert was to compare the findings of the induction with his version of the selection procedure, and to question him about the areas of interest raised by the induction. All interviews were tape-recorded and a transcript drawn up. A flow chart, based on the content of the transcript, was produced for approval by the expert. He approved the flow chart, although it was later found to have a serious omission. In fact, the expert found it easier to test rules by assessing their accuracy on actual examples rather than by examination of the rules themselves. Figure 4 is a decision tree formed from the expert's rules. An early version of this had a whole branch missing, as indicated, but the expert failed to notice this. More complex trees pose even greater problems for testing and checking. The problems of testing a system have been noted by Welbank (1983), who includes testing as a stage of elicitation.

3.5.2. Extracts from the Transcript

This section contains some extracts from the interviews. They have not been edited, apart from slight changes in details that do not affect the sense, but retain privacy of any potentially sensitive details. E stands for expert, and K for knowledge engineer.

K: First of all I'd like you to describe to me how you set about selecting . . .

E: You mean the application forms?

K: When you receive an application form you have to decide whether to reject, interview or send an offer . . .

E: When the application form comes in the overall appearance is an influence. I look at the overall appearance and if there's any questions, for example, rejections from another course or the title of our course is wrong, then I begin to get suspicious. Then I open the form and scan the qualifications list. If the student has put down a whole list of failures then I get suspicious. . . . In particular, failures in exam X make me start to look for reasons to reject, not accept. [Here the expert turned to some forms.]

E: This would be a tricky student

K: Why? He has the minimum requirements.

E: He has a weak academic background of failures. It might be countermanded by the reference. If the reference is first-rate and gives reasons as to why the previous results are not as good as they might have been, for example a problem at home. . . . then I start to overlook the faults and relook at the qualifications. If the reference, on the other hand, is not supportive then it is still a weak background. If the reference reference says even that it supports the application then there are usually sufficient grounds to accept the student in spite of discrepancies in qualifications. But if that is missing you start to feel justified in giving him a reject. Now if in addition they point out that subject Y is weak . . . then you go for a reject. This is on the basis of other people's assertions as well, not my own. So we look at the back, and if it looks as if he's having difficulty with written work then I read this carefully . . .

If the student lives a long way off then I make an offer without an interview. If they're from background A then condition A would be asked for. If they're coming in via background B then there's a very strong likelihood that they'll be accepted if there aren't any discrepancies in subject Y. This normally qualifies for a place without hesitation unless they are having obvious difficulties with Y and the reference also points this out. Background C is usually accompanied by very bad marks, and they usually get a rejection unless the reference is really praiseworthy. But even then you can't be sure. That's as much as I can think of.

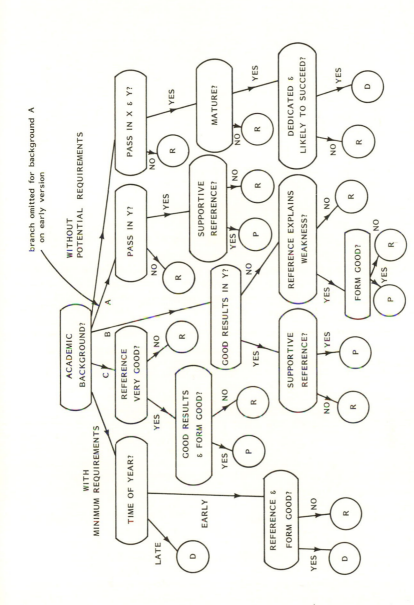

FIGURE 4. The decision tree based on the consultation with the expert. It has a different structure from that of Figure 3. The expert failed to notice that the section indicated had been omitted from an early version.

K: What about definite offers if they've already met the requirements?

E: If they've met all the entry requirements and the reference is in order and they've filled in the back of the form OK then make an offer. . . . I don't waste time interviewing people I don't want. It's highly unlikely that an interviewee will get a rejection letter, unless he's totally inarticulate . . .

K: There are cases of people without minimum requirements and no exams to be taken. What about these?

E: They may make personal contact. Usually they can sell themselves very effectively and provide reasoned evidence why they haven't got the qualifications. Effectively they can influence me by their general attitude and overall motivation.

   They would have to show me that they could complete the course. Possibly some sort of prospect at the end of the course. . . .

K: Does their age influence you at all?

E: Not usually, no.

K: So you'd treat a 19-year-old the same as a 30-year-old?

E: I think a 30-year-old would probably be on stronger ground. . . . Usually the mature students are more committed to what they're doing. A 19-year-old couldn't come in and influence you in that way.

K: Does there come a point when age or maturity can go against them?

E: Obviously if their whole demeanor and age and general circumstances indicates absolutely no chance of them getting a job at the end, then since the course book says we've got to take account of vocational prospects then they wouldn't get an offer.

K: What's the hardest type of decision you have to make?

E: Very bright nationality Z with no subject Y.

K: Is this a big problem?

E: Only because it's stipulated for me.

K: Do you get many?

E: I had one last week.

K: Do you have problems with the older ill-qualified students?

E: Sometimes I have to plead with other people to take them on.

K: But it's very straightforward in your own mind?

E: Time-consuming, but straightforward. I can make my mind up quickly, but I have to convince other people.

3.6. COMMENTS ON THE INTERVIEWS

These extracts represent a small part of the dialogue but illustrate the lack of structure in the expert's descriptions. The expert was inclined to repeat himself and even contradict himself. He found difficulty in talking in abstract terms and was happier when discussing specific examples. It is not easy to extract coherent rules from such a transcript.

His explanations were influenced by his desire to justify rejections. He had been criticized in the past, and this colored much of the discussion. He tended to ignore cases that were obviously straightforward to him, and preferred to discuss interesting problems. His view of representative or frequent was biased (Tversky and Kahneman, 1977). The expert's definition of "difficult" was different from that of the knowledge engineer.

The expert classified applications by academic background. This was not obvious from the forms, and so his rules differed from the induced rules. This can be seen by comparing Figures 3 and 4. This emphasizes the fact that the expert should play a major part in compiling the training set, otherwise he might not be confident in the induced rules. A simple rule-based expert system was written using the rules given by the expert, and in the same format as that output by the inductive program. The predictive powers of these rules were tested by running the system on all the examples used for ID3, both training and test cases. In this case the two sets of rules had almost identical success rates for prediction, but the expert believed that the rules from induction were in some way foreign.

The original statement in 3.3.1 ("If they've got the minimum requirements then I offer a place") was incorrect, and a common misuse of *if*. What he meant was "If they do not have the minimum requirements then I reject them." This statement is not true in the case of mature students, but it is closer to the truth. People often use *if* instead of *only if*; induction uses *if* logically and consistently.

When pressed to detail his decision making, the expert could not really appreciate the problem and described the speed with which he was able to act. In an instance like this, further detailed questioning is likely to result in disjoint and confused contradictions and repetitions. Experts often fail to realize that they have knowledge, let alone how they use it.

4. CONCLUSION

4.1. ISSUES IN INDUCTION

This chapter has concentrated on the ID3 algorithm. There are other algorithms (Dieterrich and Michalski, 1981). One that has been used very successfully is AQ11 (Cohen and Feigenbaum, 1982). Michalsky and Chilausky (1980) report very good results in soybean disease analysis using this. They found that results from induction were better than asking the experts to describe their diagnosis. Others have asserted that their results could not have been achieved without induction (Michie, 1985). Some of the outstanding issues are given below.

4.1.1. Evaluation

Any induced rules should be tested on examples not in the training set. Quinlan's original work does this, but some implementations omit this important aspect. If this is not an automatic part of the algorithm, then the knowledge engineer should do this himself. Claims in package documentation tend to be optimistic. The algorithm will probably produce results even in an area where it is unsuitable to do so. Most real example sets will contain uncertain data, and implementers of the algorithm should build in a method for evaluating results, particularly for the rare cases.

4.1.2. Size of Training Set

Many people ask how many examples are needed in the training set. This cannot be prescribed since it depends on the problem being investigated. This is one of the reasons why the evaluation is important: An inadequate training set will produce results that are very sensitive to changes in the training set. Sample data are 50 examples, 10 attributes, and 3 classes for this simple problem, and 215 examples, 19 attributes, and 2 classes for a more complex one (Breiman *et al.*, 1984).

4.1.3. Informative Output

The knowledge engineer needs to have confidence in the output, especially since the expert may argue that he does not follow the induced rules. Inductive aids would be more useful if they provided information about the results—e.g., any weak links in the tree, or a node where an arbitrary choice was made between the attributes where the information values were equal. Some implementations of ID3 have made such modifications to the original algorithm, but they are often inadequately documented (Hart, 1985b).

4.1.4. Pruning Trees

If data are allowed to be uncertain and inaccurate, then it is unrealistic to rely on all of the induced tree, particularly the lower nodes (Hart, 1985a). Methods of pruning trees to remove weak links and also including misclassification costs and probabilistic rules have been well documented elsewhere (Breiman *et al.*, 1984). These methods could be included as options in inductive software.

4.1.5. Real Numbers

Real attributes pose a problem because the algorithm will produce a single cutoff point for a rule. Such a rule should be discussed very carefully with the expert. There is no reason why a confidence interval for this cutoff point could not be indicated in the output. This would enable the knowledge engineer to investigate whether any misclassification was caused by uncertainty in the cutoff value or by other factors.

4.1.6. Structured Approach

A common method of tackling complex problems in systems analysis or program design is to break a large problem into smaller and more manageable subproblems. This is called a structured approach. Results tend to be better from a structured methodology, and so there is evidence that this is the way in which the brain tackles problems efficiently. A structured approach in induction involves identifying subproblems with their own training sets, and also building up these subproblems into a structure for the overall problem. This has been done in the analysis of chess (Shapiro and Niblett, 1982), and at least one implementation of ID3 has the facility built into the software (Hassan *et al.*, 1985).

Figure 5 shows a possible structure for an expert system dealing with applications for three courses, A, B, and C. There are general requirements that have to be met for these. In addition, each of the three courses has specific requirements that can be induced from three different training sets. This design also shows how there are subproblems for dealing with the reference: For courses A and B the rules are identical and different from course C. All the specific requirements are linked together to form a single expert system. This structure seems more natural than using one large training set including all the attributes from each of the subproblems.

4.1.7. Fuzzy Rules

In the case study one of the attributes was the quality of the reference. This is coded as *good, fair,* or *poor.* The classification of a particular reference requires judgment and is not solved in the induced tree of Figure 3, where the expertise for this remains with the user. As noted in 3.4, the knowledge engineer did not really find induction much help for this problem. Furthermore, the expert found it difficult to be precise about the quality of a reference. He used fuzzy terms such as *good, supportive, explain* without much inclination to explain them.

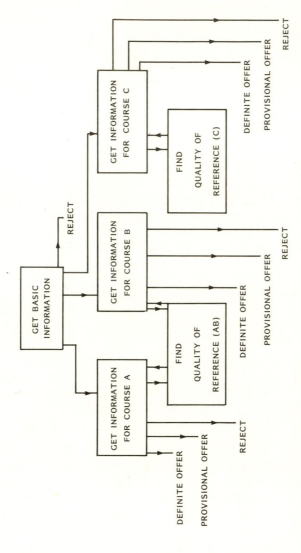

FIGURE 5. Some complex problems can be structured into subproblems. This represents an expert system designed to deal with applications for three different courses. Boxes lower down on the diagram represent subproblems requiring training sets.

This is really a subproblem within the selection procedure, and an important one. As described in 4.1.6, rules for this can be induced from a special subset of examples and attributes. The main problem is encouraging the expert to be more specific. Some techniques from psychology, e.g., the repertory grid, might prove helpful here. Alternatively, the expert could be asked to identify the key phrases in a reference that made it good or poor.

If the expert finds it difficult or impossible to define qualitative descriptors, then the knowledge engineer can experiment using induction and produce what he believes to be reasonable definitions, based on a training set, for comment by the expert. This is a further use for induction, although in this case it would be time-consuming.

4.2. GUIDELINES SUMMARY

In conclusion, the following guidelines describe the results of this study.

4.2.1. *Suitability of Domain*

Induction can be useful if there are documented examples, or if they can be obtained easily. However, knowledge domains where rules are not appropriate are unsuitable for induction. These include some real-time problems where systems are alerted by observations in an order that is unpredictable, and where reaction is required quickly.

Suitable problems include pattern recognition (for a subset of shapes), fault diagnosis, and guidance in the use of a set of procedures.

4.2.2. *Advantages*

Induction is consistent and unbiased, although it probably uses only one form of reasoning. Rules are relatively easy to understand, and the output is simpler than that from statistical packages. Unlike many statistical methods, it makes very few assumptions about the underlying distributions in the data. It is repeatable and indefatigable, and it does not make false assumptions or forget to state results as an expert might. If a training set is available, then induction is rapid, and provided that the examples are comprehensive, it can discover rules that the expert might be unaware of or be unable to express clearly. It can suggest rules and identify difficult, interesting, or contradictory cases in the training or subsequent examples. Induction discovers knowledge away from the expert, providing the knowledge engineer with results, questions, and hypotheses to form the basis of a consultation with the expert. Alternatively, the expert might find an inductive program a useful way of expressing his knowledge or experimenting with hypotheses.

4.2.3. Disadvantages

Induction usually produces results without explanations. It cannot distinguish between attributes that are necessary and those that are confirmatory. It assumes that the training set is complete and correct. There is no guarantee that the induced results are valid for examples other than those in the training set. Output needs to be evaluated critically.

4.2.4. A Training Set

The guidelines obtained from the case study describe the selection and use of the training set. The quality of the output depends on the training set, and so great attention should be paid to its composition and use. The expert should use his judgment to select attributes that seem natural to him but should not be pressed to guess or overspecify. He should also identify the different types of problems he deals with in order to define the structure of the training set. Attributes should be relevant and not highly correlated. The knowledge engineer must not be afraid to change this set if the expert agrees that the results are inadequate, but care must be taken not to impose a preconceived solution on the problem.

4.2.5. Evaluation of Output

The output must always be evaluated, preferably with both documented examples and the expert. Results should not be sensitive to small changes in the training set or particularly relevant to the chosen examples. The expert should be able to discuss the way in which attributes are used in the output: He may be able to distinguish between necessary and confirmatory attributes, and to offer explanations as to why certain attributes do not feature in the output. This discussion gives more detail of his knowledge.

5. REFERENCES

Breiman, L., Friedman, J. H., Olshen, R. A., and Stone, C. J. (1984). *Classification and regression trees.* Belmont, Calif.: Wadsworth International.

Cohen, P. R., and Feigenbaum, E. A. (Eds.). (1982). *The handbook of artificial intelligence* (Vol. 3). London: Pitman.

Dieterrich, T. G., and Michalski, R. S. (1981). Inductive learning of structural descriptions. *Artificial Intelligence, 16,* 257–294.

Feigenbaum, E. A., and McCorduck, P. (1984). *The fifth generation.* London: Pan Books.

Fox, J. (1984). Doubts about induction. In *Bulletin of SPL insight.* Abingdon, England: SPL International.

Gordon, A. D. (1981). *Classification: Methods for the exploratory analysis of multivariate data.* London: Chapman and Hall.

Hart, A. (1985a). Experience in the use of an induction system in knowledge engineering. In M. A. Bramer (Ed.), *Research and development in expert systems.* Cambridge: Cambridge University Press.

Hart, A. (1985b). The role of induction in knowledge elicitation. *Expert Systems, 2,* 24–28.

Hassan, T., A-Razzak, M., Michie, D., and Pettipher, R. (1985). EX-TRAN 7: A different approach for an expert system generator: *Proceedings of the fifth international workshop on expert systems and their applications,* Avignon, France.

Jackson, P. (1985). Reasoning about belief in the context of advice-giving systems. In M. A. Bramer (Ed.), *Research and development in expert systems.* Cambridge: Cambridge University Press.

Kidd, A., and Welbank, M. (1984). Knowledge acquisition. In J. Fox (Ed.), *Expert systems.* Infotech State of the Art Report. Oxford: Pergamon Infotech Ltd.

Kullback, S. (1967). *Information theory and statistics.* New York: Dover.

Michalski, R. S., and Chilausky, R. L. (1980). Knowledge acquisition by encoding expert rules versus computer induction from examples—A case study involving soybean pathology. *International Journal of Man-Machine Studies, 12,* 63–87.

Michie, D. (1985). Expert systems interview. *Expert Systems, 2,* 20–23.

Michie, D., and Johnston, R. (1985). *The creative computer.* London, England: Pelican.

Quinlan, R. (1979). Discovering rules from large collections of examples: A case study. In D. Michie (Ed.), *Expert systems in the microelectronic age.* Edinburgh: Edinburgh University Press.

Shapiro, A., and Niblett, T. (1982). Automatic induction of classification rules for a chess endgame. In M. R. B. Clarke, *Advances in computer chess.* Oxford: Pergamon Press.

Sneath, P. H., and Sokal, R. R. (1973). *Numerical taxonomy.* San Francisco: Freeman.

Tversky, A., and Kahneman, D. (1977). Judgement under uncertainty: Heuristics and biases. In P. N. Johnson-Laird and P. C. Watson (Eds.), *Thinking: Readings in cognitive science.* Cambridge: Cambridge University Press.

Welbank, M. (1983). *A review of knowledge acquisition techniques for expert systems.* Ipswich: British Telecommunications, Martlesham Consultancy Services.

Index